Potjiekos from Huisgenoot

Potjiekos from Huisgenoot

Marlene Hammann

Human & Rousseau
Cape Town   Johannesburg

The publication of this book at a reasonable price
has been made possible by a contribution from
Culemborg Wines

First edition, first impression 1987
Second impression 1988
Second edition (Limp cover) 1990
Second impression 1993
Third impression 1994
Fourth impression 1994
Fifth impression 1995
Sixth impression 1996

Copyright © 1987 strictly reserved
English translation by Cecilia van Zyl
Published by Human & Rousseau (Pty.) Ltd.
State Building, 3-9 Rose Street, Cape Town
Photography by David Briers
Dishes styled for photography by Danielle Boschi
Drawings by Louwra Marais
Typography and cover design by Etienne van Duyker
Typeset in 10 on 11 pt Souvenir Light by Studiographix
Printed and bound by National Book Printers,
Drukkery Street, Goodwood, Western Cape

ISBN 0 7981 2785 6

Contents

Preface

The idea materialised with *Huisgenoot's* seventieth birthday in 1986: to have a potjiekos shindig for everyone who enjoys a good potjie. Three competitions and some superb get-togethers later, *Huisgenoot* had collected the cream of the country's potjiekos recipes. However, not even a splendid supplement in *Huisgenoot* could do them justice. In order to preserve these recipes for the potjiekos fraternity, it became evident that we would have to publish them in book form.

And so it became my gastronomical privilege to test and organise the recipes from this book. A special thank you to all my fellow enthusiasts whose names appear alongside the many excellent recipes in this collection. Thank you also to Denise Loeblich and Estelle Crowson who helped me with the daunting task of testing the recipes.

And of course, I cannot neglect to mention our families who so obligingly submitted themselves to a diet of potjiekos for weeks on end – not that they ever really had reason to complain!

Finally, a very special thank you to Colonel D.W. van Rooyen, Chairman of the Northern Transvaal Potjiekos Guild, the body which unremittingly dedicates itself to the standardisation of competitions. He provided us with a wealth of invaluable information on the preparation of potjiekos which we have included in the introductory chapter, as well as casting an approving eye over the final manuscript.

We're convinced that *Potjiekos from Huisgenoot* will be warmly welcomed by the potjiekos fraternity. This book is, after all, the result of a team effort in the best potjie tradition.

Marlene Hammann

How to prepare potjiekos

The greatest triumph for any cook worth his salt, is an appreciative response to his culinary efforts. Nothing beats the warm glow of pride and satisfaction of seeing empty plates eagerly passed back for seconds.

This sense of achievement is no less for those who belong to that special breed of cooks who can stir up a meal fit for a king in a humble three-legged, round-bellied little black pot.

Ah, what bliss to see friends and family mopping up every morsel as they partake of your fragrant offerings. "What's the secret?" they ask in between mouthfuls. And you simply smile quietly to yourself and say: "Go on, have another potato."

Because you know very well that the secret ingredient for a good potjie is first and foremost loving care.

And this no one person can teach another. Fortunately though, one can learn the skills of preparing sublime potjiekos. Which is exactly what is contained in this book – proven expertise to initiate you into the secrets of the little black pot. And hopefully this will inspire you to prepare the most delectable potjie meals for your friends and family . . . in the true potjiekos tradition of warmth and friendship.

But for those of us who are less moved by the romantic spirit of the potjie, let me hasten to add that there's hardly a more economical way of entertaining, the reason being that the potjie invariably calls for the less expensive meat cuts.

So how does one get the pot boiling?

By purchasing your own pot and breaking it in, of course. Once we've covered that ritual, we'll let you into the secrets of stoking up the fire, and finally we'll move on to the actual preparation of the potjie.

And so you'll come to join the ranks of those who unashamedly admit to indulging in an overriding passion for the delights of the three-legged, round-bellied little black pot!

The potjie

Firstly, what size pot do you require? For the average family of four to six a no. 3 pot is just about right. Before buying your pot, inspect it carefully for any cracks and ensure that the lid seals properly.

Once you've brought your precious pot home, scour the inside thoroughly using either wood ash or sandpaper. Grease both the inside and outside with pork fat. Your pot is now ready to be "cooked in". The scouring and "cooking in" processes are most important to prevent your food from having an iron taste or from being contaminated by a black deposit.

Fill the pot with a slack mealie meal porridge mixture and allow it to simmer over a slow fire for a few hours. Leftover vegetables or peels and even boiled fat, obtainable from your butcher, can be used instead of mealie meal porridge. Repeat the process a few times to ensure that the pot has been thoroughly "cooked in".

Now coat the inside of the pot with a thin layer of fat or cooking oil to prevent it from rusting, and put it away until needed. Rinse the pot with warm soapy water after every potjiekos meal. And don't forget that layer of oil or fat. The more frequently the pot is used, the smoother and shinier its inside will become, and the easier it will be to clean.

The fire

The fire, as Colonel D.W. van Rooyen of the Northern Transvaal Potjiekos Guild so aptly remarks, can either make or break a potjie. Beginners are inclined to stoke too big a fire, resulting in burnt offerings.

Remember, a good potjie refuses to be rushed. Haste and impatience cannot be reconciled with the peaceful *gemütlichkeit* that descends round a potjie. All that's required is enough heat to quietly let it simmer away. In the meantime, you can keep a keen ear tuned to the bubbling of your pot. You will eventually be able to recognise its characteristic sound.

But what about rainy days when a fire is out of the question, or if you have no access to alfresco cooking facilities? Granted, some potjiekos fanatics will be horrified at the idea of cooking potjiekos on a gas stove. Others think it rather unfair to limit this tradition to the conventional fireside gathering.

Potjiekos cooked on a gas stove (in the kitchen or even placed in the hearth, if possible) has all the makings of an equally pleasurable and entertaining gathering. Some gas stoves even come equipped with a special ring in which to place a three-legged pot. (Or what about a potjie placed over a wood or charcoal fire in the fireplace on a cold winter's day? Potjiekos fanatics are, after all, noted for their unlimited fund of resourceful ideas!)

However, to regulate the coals of an open fire is not as simple as regulating the flame of a gas stove. So it's worth one's while to heed the advice of the experts when it comes to the lighting of the potjie fire.

Any hard wood will do, including charcoal. It is also useful to have a second fire going as well from which you can replenish the first with hot coals if need be.

Take care not to have too many coals burning directly under the pot. Rather arrange the coals around the pot. This will enable you to regulate the fire more efficiently by moving the coals further away from or

10

closer to the pot. A small spade comes in very handy to this chore.

And remember, fresh herbs like rosemary or thyme sprinkled on the coals every now and then, perfume the air around the potjie with their own special fragrance.

The level at which the fire is made, is another important aspect for some potjiekos fundis. Those with long legs will obviously prefer their potjies at a slightly higher level than their shorter fellow enthusiasts – bending over a too low pot can be killing on the back.

Because potjiekos takes a while to cook, good timing is essential. Decide on what time you would like to serve your potjie and then calculate in reverse to determine when you should start the fire. This in itself takes quite some time, while the preparation and simmering of your pot will, of course, add a good few hours.

You can rest assured that it will take four to eight hours before a meat potjie is done to a turn, while a chicken and a fish potjie will respectively take about three hours and one hour before it's ready. In the meantime, pass some snacks around to keep the hunger pangs at bay! After all, the intention of a potjiekos get-together is to allow for plenty of unhurried, companionable togetherness.

Preparing the potjie

It makes good sense to calculate how much meat and vegetables will be required per person. Approximately 300 grams meat with bones (200 grams without bones) is recommended per person. Feel free to experiment and to adapt the recipes. At this stage you should also decide on the marinade.

Cut up your meat in pieces of the required size, peel the vegetables and keep in water (remember to add sugar to the sweet potatoes and pumpkin, and salt to the other vegetables). Then mix the marinade.

Next, wash your potjie to remove the layer of fat. Then light the fire, tending it until you have sufficient coals.

Place the potjie over the coals to heat it, but be careful of overheating. Add a dash of cooking oil to the pot, and once it is hot, add the meat.

Stir the meat around in order to coat the pot thoroughly with oil, and fry with the onions to seal in the flavour. It is advisable to fry the meat first in order to seal it and then stew it. Cook the meat in a little marinade until nearly done.

Arrange the vegetables in layers according to the cooking time each requires. Carrots will be placed at the very bottom, followed by sweet potatoes, potatoes, pumpkin, mushrooms, etc.

The vegetables should be arranged in layers and against the sides of the potjie, forming a hollow in the centre for rice. This will also prevent the rice from burning.

The marinade or liquid (water or wine) can now be added. Do not add cold liquid all at once as this will toughen the meat. Rather add it gradually by pouring it against the side of the pot, or add little by little until ± 2 cm under the top layer of vegetables.

Replace the lid and DO NOT STIR THE POT AFTER THIS, unless otherwise specified.

The heat should now be well regulated by scraping away the coals – the marinade should just be at simmering point. It's advisable to have a fork handy with which to test if the vegetables are done.

When the potjie is ready, stir it through once to ensure that the meat and vegetables at the very bottom will be dished up.

And now all that remains is to enjoy. Potjiekos is fit for a king!

Wine hints from Culemborg

While on the subject of wine, a little background knowledge is useful when selecting a wine that will do your special potjie justice.

White wines

White wines are bottled while still young and therefore retain their fruity flavour and delicate bouquet. They are the perfect accompaniment with fish, seafood and white meat potjies. Potjies with a more robust flavour (e.g. curry dishes) go well with a Late Harvest.

White wines are best served when slightly chilled. Use long-stemmed glasses to prevent your hands from warming up the contents.

Wines should never be subjected to shock treatment by freezing them.

Red wines

Red wines are best complemented by the richer red meat potjies, e.g. oxtail, shank or venison potjies. The characteristic astringency that red wines absorb from the husks help to "neutralise" the richness of these potjies.

Red wines are always served at room temperature, i.e. 16°C (60°F). If they are too cold, warm them up by wrapping the bottles in heated cloths; on warm summer days they can be slightly chilled.

Blanc de Noir wines

This type of wine can be served with both rich and light dishes as they are somewhere between white and red wines in character, although they tend to be closer to the whites. As is the case with white wines, a Blanc de Noir is always served chilled.

Other handy hints

1. If you pour a thin layer of salad oil over any leftover dry table wine and cork the bottle, it will keep for several days as a cooking wine.

2. Always heat wine before adding it to food – this will prevent the cooking process from being interrupted or the fat from coagulating.
3. During the hot summer months, do not hesitate to add soda water to wine – it is, after all, a centuries-old tradition in Europe.
4. Keep all dry wines horizontally in your cellar, which should be cool and dark.
5. If the cork is too big for the bottle, do not try and trim it down. Rather place it in boiling water for a few minutes to "shrink" it.
6. In order to tenderise any kind of meat or to enhance its flavour, soak it in wine for an hour or two before cooking.
7. Always allow wine to "rest" in the bottle if it has been transported or shaken around.
8. Although food with wine may be prepared in aluminium pots, they are unsuitable for marinating. Rather use a porcelain, enamel or glass dish for this purpose.
9. To remove stains from polished wood, rub well with a moist rag dipped in cigarette ash. Polish afterwards.
10. If any alcohol has been spilt on a carpet, sponge the stain immediately with a cloth wrung out in lukewarm, soapy water. Do not soak the carpet. Wipe, using a clean, damp cloth and brush up the pile while still damp.
11. To remove wine stains from linen, sprinkle the cloth with salt as soon as possible. Stretch the stained area over a dish, and pour boiling water on from a height of approximately 1 metre.
12. If the material cannot be washed, sprinkle the stains with flour or fuller's earth, and leave to draw in, brush out and repeat the process.

Poultry potjies

Joghurt and chicken potjie

This tasty potjie, a firm favourite with the Van Rooyens of Garsfontein, Pretoria, won them the first prize at the Northern Transvaal potjiekos competition. The lemon peel adds zest to the dish. Mashed potato or rice is an excellent accompaniment as the potjie renders a delicious gravy. The recipe serves 6-8 people and we recommend a no. 3 pot.

Marinade

500 ml natural yoghurt
500 ml dry white wine
10 ml dried thyme
10 ml grated lemon peel
1 large onion, finely chopped
5 ml freshly ground black pepper
3 bay leaves
5 ml dried tarragon

2 kg chicken pieces
2 green peppers
300 g carrots, peeled and sliced
6 large potatoes, peeled and quartered
100 g dried apricots
200 g green beans, sliced
150 g fresh mushrooms, sliced
salt to taste
1 packet mushroom soup powder (if required)

Mix all the marinade ingredients, pour over the chicken and marinade for 6-8 hours.

Heat the pot until very hot. Remove the chicken from the marinade and fry a few pieces at a time with the pepper until golden brown.

Arrange the carrots, potatoes, apricots, green beans and mushrooms in layers on top of the meat. Sprinkle with salt and add the marinade. Replace the lid and simmer slowly for 2 hours. Should the potjie render too much liquid, it can be thickened with the mushroom soup powder. Mix the soup powder with the gravy and allow to simmer for another 15 minutes.

> **Most important hint**
> *Do not stir!*

15

Chicken and noodle potjie

This delicious recipe was sent in by Mr L.J. Schroeder of Wellington. It's so filling that no accompaniments other than a mixed salad is necessary. The recipe serves 4-6 people and we recommend a no. 2 pot.

8 chicken thighs
salt and pepper to taste
30 ml cooking oil
2 celery sticks, chopped
2 tomatoes, skins removed and sliced
1 green pepper, finely sliced
250 g whole button mushrooms
250 ml chives, chopped
500 ml uncooked shell noodles
15 ml parsley, finely chopped
10 ml dried mixed herbs
5 ml freshly ground black pepper
3 ml dried rosemary
250 ml dry white wine
250 ml grated Cheddar cheese

Sprinkle the chicken with salt and pepper. Heat the oil in the pot and fry the chicken, a few pieces at a time, until golden brown.

Arrange the vegetables in layers on top of the meat in the following order: celery, tomatoes, green pepper, mushrooms and chives. Sprinkle the parsley and mixed herbs on top and add the noodles. Sprinkle the pepper and rosemary on top and pour over the wine. Cover and simmer for 1 hour.

Sprinkle with cheese and simmer for a further 20 minutes.

Photo
Piquant chicken potjie
(p. 22)

16

Tangy chicken potjie

If you like Mexican food, you'll keep on coming back for more of this chicken potjie of Johan Voges of Vredendal. The dish owes its unusual flavour to the herbs and piquant spices, and it is so filling that you only need a mixed salad as a side dish. The recipe serves 6 people and we recommend a no. 3 pot.

30 mℓ cooking oil
2 kg chicken, cut into portions
5 medium onions, chopped
1 large chili, seeded and chopped
250 mℓ water
5 carrots, peeled and sliced into strips
6 medium potatoes, peeled and cubed
125 mℓ uncooked rice
200 g frozen green peas
15 whole button mushrooms
2 tomatoes, skinned and cubed
10 mℓ dried parsley
5 mℓ garlic flakes
5 mℓ lemon pepper
5 mℓ dried oregano
2,5 mℓ coarsely ground black pepper
1,25 mℓ piri-piri powder
125 mℓ dry white wine
30 mℓ sugar
20 mℓ salt
15 mℓ mild curry powder
1 chicken stock cube, crumbled

Heat the oil in the potjie. Fry the chicken, a few pieces at a time, until golden brown. Remove and set aside. Fry the onion and chili until tender. Return the chicken to the pot and add the water. Cover and simmer for 15 minutes.

Arrange the vegetables and rice in layers on top of the meat in the order as listed. Sprinkle the herbs and spices on top and simmer for another 15 minutes.

Mix the wine with the remaining ingredients and pour over the potjiekos. Cover and simmer for 30 minutes. Check that the rice is done. If not, simmer until cooked. Stir through before serving.

Photo
Mutton potjie (p. 30)

Arthur's turkey and spaghetti potjie

Arthur Belcher and his wife Lydia of Bothasig in the Cape won a second prize in *Huisgenoot's* potjiekos competition for this delicious potjie, and in 1986 they walked off with the first prize at the Boland Agricultural Show. Lydia's raisin and aniseed pot bread (p.76) is the perfect accompaniment. The recipe serves 6-8 people and we recommend a no. 3 pot.

1 medium turkey
1 rasher of bacon, cut into small squares
a few whole cloves or coriander seeds
4 onions, chopped
30 mℓ cooking oil
salt to taste
1,2 mℓ dried rosemary
a knife-point each of the following: dried thyme, dried basil, dried oregano, paprika, chicken seasoning
boiling water
6 carrots, peeled and sliced
4 cloves garlic, crushed
4 green pepper rings
1 sprig fresh parsley, chopped
a bay leaf, broken into bits
1 piece dried orange peel
1 pack (500 g) spaghetti
200 g fresh mushrooms, sliced

Cheese sauce

60 mℓ butter or margarine
100 mℓ cake flour
1 ℓ fresh milk
500 mℓ grated Cheddar cheese

Pierce holes into the turkey and stuff each one with a piece of bacon, cloves or coriander. Marinate the meat overnight in a marinade of your own choice.

Sauté the remaining bacon and two of the onions in a little cooking oil. Remove and set aside. Cut the turkey into portions and fry in the oil until brown. Return the bacon and onion mixture to the pot with the meat.

Add the salt, rosemary, thyme, basil, oregano, paprika and chicken seasoning and enough boiling water to prevent the meat from burning. Cover and allow the potjie to simmer over the coals for approximately 1 hour or until the meat is tender. Remove the meat and debone it.

Fry the remaining two onions, carrots and garlic in the pot. Add the pepper, parsley, bay leaf and orange peel as well as the meat mixture.

Allow to simmer for another 30 minutes, taking care that it does not burn.

When the carrots are tender, remove the mixture from the pot and allow it to cool.

In the meantime, cook the spaghetti according to the instructions on the pack until it is tender and prepare the cheese sauce. Melt the butter or margarine and stir in the flour. Add the milk gradually, stirring the mixture continually until it reaches boiling point. Add the cheese.

Place a layer of cooked spaghetti, a layer of turkey and half of the cheese sauce in a greased flat-bottomed pot. Add the remaining spaghetti and turkey and on top of that, the mushrooms and remaining cheese sauce. Sprinkle a little extra grated cheese op top. Replace the lid and allow the potjie to bake among the coals for another 20 minutes. As is the case with a pot bread, place a few coals on the lid as well.

Chicken and vegetable potjie

Jeremy Punt of Stellenbosch is responsible for this mouthwatering chicken and vegetable potjie. Because the cabbage renders a lot of water, one should not add too much liquid. Mutton chops can be used instead of chicken. Serve with pearl wheat or a pot bread. The recipe serves 4-6 people and we recommend a no. 3 pot.

30 mℓ cooking oil or butter
10 chicken thighs
2 large onions, chopped
45 mℓ chutney
10 mℓ salt
5 mℓ dried mixed herbs
5 mℓ garlic flakes
1,2 mℓ freshly ground black pepper
6 large carrots, peeled and sliced
12 whole baby potatoes, peeled
1 small head of cabbage, shredded
½ medium butternut, sliced
1 tin (410 g) mealie kernels (do not drain)
125 mℓ sweet white wine

Heat the oil or butter in the pot. Fry the chicken pieces and onion together for approximately 30 minutes. Mix the chutney, salt, herbs, garlic flakes and pepper. Spread the meat evenly with half the chutney mixture. Arrange the carrots, potatoes, cabbage and butternut in layers on top of the meat. Spread evenly with the remaining chutney mixture and sprinkle the mealie kernels on top. Add the wine and allow to simmer very slowly for 1½-2 hours.

> **Hint**
> A three-legged, round-bellied pot is just perfect for potjiekos. However, a flat-bottomed pot can be used instead. Be careful to raise it slightly to prevent the coals from burning the food.

19

Potjie with chicken, broccoli and rice

Marilyn Wilken of Dewetsdorp sent in the recipe for this easy-to-prepare potjie. As a variation, sweet red wine can be used instead of the white wine. Serve with a mixed salad. The recipe serves 4-6 people and we recommend a no. 3 pot.

45 mℓ cooking oil
12 chicken thighs
flavour enhancer (e.g. Aromat)
4-6 whole cloves
6 carrots, peeled and sliced
300 g broccoli, broken into florets
300 g whole button mushrooms
250 g courgettes, thickly sliced
250 mℓ uncooked rice
5 mℓ salt
1 ℓ boiling water
2 chicken stock cubes
125 mℓ dry white wine
30 mℓ mushroom soup powder, mixed with 125 mℓ cold water

Heat the oil in the pot. Season the chicken pieces with flavour enhancer and fry a few pieces at a time until golden brown. Return all the meat to the pot and add the cloves. Cover and allow to simmer for 30 minutes.

Arrange the vegetables in layers on top of the meat in the order as listed. Make a hollow in the centre and place the rice and salt in it. Dissolve the chicken stock cube in the boiling water and add to the pot. Replace the lid and allow to simmer very slowly for 1½ hours without stirring.

Add the wine and mushroom soup, replace the lid and simmer for a further 10 minutes.

Chicken and mushroom potjie

This delicious chicken potjie of Deon van Eeden of Vredendal was a sure-fire hit in our household. The secret lies in the fact that no liquid is added – the ingredients are cooked in their own natural juices. Even the rice requires no extra liquid for cooking. Because few vegetables are used, a mixed salad is an excellent accompaniment. The recipe serves 12 people and we recommend a no. 6 pot.

200 g butter
3 kg chicken pieces
8 medium onions, sliced
6 medium potatoes, peeled and cut into small pieces
250 g rindless streaky bacon, cut into small pieces
900 g whole button mushrooms
1 tin (440 g) pineapple chunks, drained
1 packet RiceOMix, chicken flavour
25 mℓ chicken seasoning
5 mℓ Worcester sauce
5 mℓ salt
5 mℓ freshly ground black pepper

Heat the pot and melt a knob of butter in it. Fry the chicken, a few pieces at a time, until golden brown. Melt the remaining butter, add the onions, cover and steam for 10 minutes until nearly done.

Add the chicken to the onions in the pot, replace the lid and simmer for 45 minutes. Add the potatoes and simmer for 30 minutes until tender.

Arrange the bacon, mushrooms, pineapple and rice in layers on top of the potatoes. Add the chicken seasoning and Worcester sauce. Sprinkle with salt and pepper to taste. Replace the lid and simmer for another hour until the rice is done.

Delicious chicken potjie

Hint

Remove any superfluous fat from meat, especially chicken, or else you'll end up with a greasy gravy. If the meat is very fatty, add an extra potato or two.

One would never guess that this tasty chicken potjie, created by Mr O.J. Oelofse of Germiston South, is so economical. It goes well with a green salad like green bean salad. The recipe serves 4 people and we recommend a no. 2 pot.

45 mℓ cooking oil
1 kg chicken thighs
10 mℓ salt
4 bay leaves
pinch dried thyme
4 black pepper corns
pinch ground allspice
45 mℓ chutney
500 mℓ carrots, peeled and sliced
6 large potatoes, peeled and sliced
500 g whole button mushrooms
125 mℓ boiling water
1 chicken stock cube

Heat the oil in the pot. Sprinkle the thighs with salt and fry the chicken, a few pieces at a time, until golden brown.

Add the herbs, spices and chutney. Arrange the carrots, potatoes and mushrooms in layers on top of the chicken. Dissolve the stock cube in the water and add it to the potjie. Replace the lid and simmer for approximately 1 hour and 20 minutes. Should the potjie become too dry, add a little water.

Piquant chicken potjie

If you like piquant dishes, you will rave about this potjie of Mr P. Serfontein of Kuils River. A pot bread, pot dumplings or rice is an excellent accompaniment for mopping up the flavoursome gravy. The recipe serves 4 people and we recommend a no. 2 pot.

1 braai pack chicken
salt and pepper to taste
5 mℓ dried thyme
2 medium onions, sliced
2 medium sweet potatoes, peeled and sliced
250 g dried peaches, soaked overnight in 375 ml water

Sauce

200 mℓ tomato sauce	
125 mℓ sunflower oil	
30 mℓ vinegar	
15 mℓ Worcester sauce	
10 mℓ paprika	
5 mℓ chopped garlic	
5 mℓ salt	
5 mℓ cayenne pepper	
4 drops of Tobasco sauce	

Heat the pot well. In the meantime, season the chicken pieces with salt, pepper and thyme. Place the chicken in the pot. Drain the peaches, saving the water. Arrange the onions, sweet potatoes and peaches in layers on top of the meat. Add the peach water and cover. Simmer gently for approximately 30 minutes.

In the meantime, mix all the ingredients for the gravy and add to the potjie. Replace the lid and simmer for 1½ hours.

Chicken and pork potjie

No wonder this colourful potjie is a favourite of Mr O.J. Oelofse of Germiston South. The apricot jam imparts a wonderful flavour. Serve with rice or mashed potatoes. The recipe serves 4-5 people and a no. 2 pot is recommended.

45 mℓ cooking oil	
1 kg chicken drumsticks	
500 g pork, cubed	
salt and pepper to taste	
3 large onions, sliced	
2 green peppers, seeded and cut into rings	
8 whole cloves	
45 mℓ smooth apricot jam	
500 mℓ green beans, sliced	
375 mℓ semi-dry white wine	
3 medium tomatoes, skinned and sliced	

Heat the oil in the pot. Sprinkle the chicken and pork with salt and pepper. Fry the meat gently, a few pieces at a time, until golden brown. Remove and set aside.

Sauté the onion and green pepper for a few minutes and add the cloves. Return the meat and chicken to the pot and spread the chicken with the jam. Add the beans and wine, cover and simmer for 45 minutes.

Add the tomatoes and simmer for a further 45 minutes.

Chicken potjie in a cream sauce

This potjie has the most sublime rich and creamy sauce with a chicken and bacon flavour. The recipe was sent in by Veronica Wium of Malmesbury. If you think the dish might be too rich, substitute half the cream for milk. Serve with rice or a pot bread. The recipe serves 4-6 people and we recommend a no. 2 pot.

6 chicken thighs
barbecue spice to taste
250 g rindless breakfast bacon, cut into small pieces
4 medium onions, chopped
60 ml smooth apricot jam
100 ml water
15 ml Worcester sauce
12 whole button onions, peeled
10 whole baby potatoes, peeled
750 ml frozen mixed vegetables
300 g mushrooms, sliced
flavour enhancer (e.g. Aromat) according to taste
1 packet oxtail soup powder
1 packet thick white onion soup powder
500 ml fresh cream or 250 ml cream and 250 ml milk

Sprinkle the chicken with barbecue spice. Heat the pot and fry the bacon for 5 minutes. Add the onions and apricot jam and fry until the onions are tender.

Add the chicken, water and Worcester sauce to the onion mixture. Cover and simmer for 15 minutes. Add the onions and potatoes and simmer for a further 10 minutes.

Add the vegetables and mushrooms next. Sprinkle with flavour enhancer, replace the lid and simmer for 30 minutes.

Mix the soup powders with the cream and add to the potjie. Allow to simmer for 30 minutes.

Chicken with apricots and almonds

The recipe for this typical Malay chicken potjie was sent in by Miss N.J. van Niekerk of Benoni. It's a most unusual potjie which is sure to become a firm favourite. Serve with yellow rice. The recipe serves 4-6 people and we recommend a no. 2 pot.

30 mℓ cooking oil	
1 large chicken, cut into portions	
3 medium onions, chopped	
2 green peppers, seeded and sliced into strips	
5 mℓ ground ginger	
2 cloves garlic, finely chopped	
2 cardamom seeds, slightly crushed	
1 cinnamon stick	
1 tin (410 g) whole tomatoes, chopped	
5 mℓ salt	
2,5 mℓ saffron	
250 mℓ boiling water	
50 g dried apricots, soaked in water and drained	
15 mℓ cornflour	
100 g almond slivers	

Heat the oil in the pot. Sauté the onions, peppers, ginger, garlic, cardamom seeds and cinnamon stick until the onions are tender. Add the chicken portions and fry gently. Add the tomatoes with their juice and salt to the chicken. Cover and simmer over a medium heat for 45 minutes, or until the chicken is tender.

Soak the saffron in the boiling water for approximately 30 minutes. Add the saffron water, apricots and cornflour to the potjie and stir well. Cover and simmer for 15 minutes or until the apricots are tender. Sprinkle with almond slivers before serving.

Meat potjies

Have-some-more neck of mutton and vegetable potjie

This great potjie was created by Mias and Anna Bouwer of Excelsior in the Free State. It not only tastes good, but looks so good it'll make your mouth water! Serve a pot bread as a side dish. The recipe serves 6 people, and we recommend a no. 3 pot.

30 mℓ butter
12 pieces neck of mutton
4 medium onions, chopped
250 mℓ water
6 black peppercorns
4 bay leaves
3 whole cloves
15 mℓ salt
15 mℓ flavour enhancer (e.g. Aromat)
10 mℓ dried parsley
2,5 mℓ coarsely ground black pepper
500 g whole baby carrots, peeled
15 medium potatoes, peeled and quartered
500 g cauliflower, broken into florets
500 g whole button mushrooms
6 courgettes, thickly sliced
4 tomatoes, skinned and chopped
500 g dried peaches and prunes, soaked in water for 1 hour and drained
90 mℓ brown gravy powder, dissolved in 125 mℓ water
250 mℓ dry white wine

Heat the pot and melt the butter. Brown the meat on both sides a few pieces at a time. Remove and set aside. Fry the onions until tender. Return the meat to the pot and add the water, peppercorns, bay leaves, cloves and 10 mℓ salt. Cover and simmer for approximately 1 hour.

In the meantime, mix the flavour enhancer, parsley, pepper and 5 mℓ salt. Arrange the vegetables in layers in the order as listed and sprinkle the mixed seasoning in between the layers. Arrange the dried fruit on top. Replace the lid and simmer for about 1½ hours.

Add the wine and dissolved brown gravy powder and simmer for another 30 minutes until done.

Mutton and bacon potjie

Amanda Prinsloo of Bredasdorp sent us the recipe for this creamy potjie. It's so delicious, it's meant for sharing with friends! Because the potjie has a slightly sour taste, beer griddle cakes (see p. 78) will do it justice. If you use apricots, the potjie will have an even more sour taste. The recipe serves 6 people and we recommend a no. 2 pot.

30 ml margarine or butter
2 medium onions, thinly sliced
250 g rindless bacon, chopped
10 ml barbecue spice
salt and pepper to taste
1 kg neck of mutton, cut in pieces
300 ml dry white wine
150 ml water
50 ml Worcester sauce
150 g dried peaches or apricots, soaked in water for 1 hour and drained
3 large carrots, peeled and sliced
5 medium potatoes, peeled and halved
250 g courgettes, sliced
200 g whole button mushrooms

Sauce
200 ml fresh milk
100 ml fresh cream
30 ml apricot jam
30 ml cornflour

Heat the pot and melt the butter in it. Fry the onions until tender, remove and set aside. Fry the bacon until crisp, remove and set aside. Season the meat with salt, pepper and spices and brown lightly on both sides. Mix the wine, water and Worcester sauce and add just enough to cover the meat. Cover and simmer gently for 1½ hours.

Add the dried peaches or apricots, carrots, bacon and onions. Replace the lid and simmer for 15 minutes. Arrange the potatoes, courgettes and mushrooms in layers on top. Cover and simmer for a further 15 minutes. Add the remaining liquid, replace the lid and simmer for approximately 1 hour.

Mix the milk, cream and jam with the cornflour and add. Simmer for 20 minutes.

> **Hint**
> Brandy is excellent for tenderising the toughest meat.

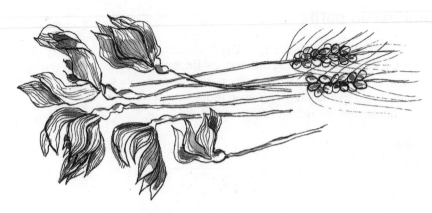

Waterblommetjie potjie

This typical South African potjie recipe was sent in by Danie Jooste of Bloemfontein. It's a recipe that comes in handy when the days become colder, as it should ideally be made with fresh waterblommetjies which are available at the beginning of winter. Serve with rice. The recipe freezes well. It serves 6 people and we recommend a no. 2 or 3 pot.

1 kg waterblommetjies
45 ml cooking oil
1 kg neck of mutton, cut into pieces
500 g mutton shank, cubed
3 medium onions, finely chopped
250 ml dry white wine
1 l water
83 ml pearl wheat
6 medium potatoes, peeled and quartered
2 cooking apples, peeled and cubed
2,5 ml lemon pepper
juice of half a lemon
salt to taste

Wash the waterblommetjies thoroughly and soak them in salt water for about 2 hours. Drain and remove the stems.

Heat the oil in the pot. Brown the meat a few pieces at a time in the pot and remove. Add the onions to the pot and fry gently until tender. Return the meat to the pot and add salt to taste. Add the wine and water. Cover and simmer for approximately 1¼ hours.

Place the pearl wheat on top of the meat, cover and simmer for 30 minutes.

Arrange the waterblommetjies, potatoes and apples in layers on top. Simmer for another 1 hour. Add the seasoning. Add salt to taste and simmer for another 30 minutes.

Neck of mutton and vegetable potjie

Fanie Linde of Excelsior in the Free State sent us this recipe. With a potjie pearl wheat as a side dish, your guests will feast until only the bare bones remain. The recipe serves 4 people and we recommend a no. 2 pot.

30 mℓ cooking oil	
6 pieces neck of mutton	
600 mℓ water	
2 medium onions, sliced	
salt and pepper to taste	
10 mℓ dried parsley	
6 whole black peppercorns	
5 mℓ barbecue spice	
5 mℓ flavour enhancer (e.g. Aromat)	
2 whole cloves	
2 celery sticks, sliced	
250 mℓ whole baby carrots, peeled	
6 medium potatoes, peeled and halved	
250 mℓ cauliflower, broken into florets	
1 tomato, skinned and sliced	
250 mℓ broccoli, broken into florets	
250 mℓ mixed dried fruit, soaked in water for 1 ½ hours and drained	
12 whole button mushrooms	
250 mℓ dry white wine	
1 packet oxtail soup powder	

Heat the oil in the pot and brown the meat. Add 250 mℓ water to the meat and cover. Simmer for 1 hour.

Mix the salt, pepper, herbs and spices well. Add half the onions to the pot as well as half the herbs and spices mixture. Cover and simmer for another 15 minutes.

Arrange the vegetables in layers on top of the meat in the following order, placing the remaining onions between the layers: celery, carrots, potatoes, cauliflower, tomato, broccoli, dried fruit and mushrooms. Sprinkle the remaining herbs and spices mixture on top. Add 250 mℓ of the water and the wine and replace the lid. Simmer gently for 2½ hours.

Mix the soup powder with the remaining water 30 minutes before serving and add to the potjie.

Hint
Too many tomatoes or too much dried fruit dominates the other ingredients and results in a too sour potjie.

Mutton potjie

Mr A.D. Labuschagne of Mondeor, Johannesburg, sent in the recipe for this potjie with its unusual assortment of vegetable flavours. Serve with rice or whole-wheat bread. The recipe serves 4 people and we recommend a no. 2 pot.

30 mℓ cooking oil
1 kg mutton shank, cut into pieces
1 large onion, chopped
100 g tomato purée
10 mℓ white sugar
375 mℓ water
6 black peppercorns
4 bay leaves
salt to taste
250 g whole baby carrots, peeled
3 medium potatoes, peeled and halved
200 g cauliflower, broken into florets
250 g courgettes, thickly sliced
100 g frozen green peas

Gravy

250 mℓ cold water
20 mℓ flour
10 mℓ brown gravy powder (e.g. Bisto)

Heat the oil in the pot and brown the meat on both sides. Remove the meat and set aside. Fry the onions until tender. Return the meat to the pot. Mix the tomato purée, sugar and water and add to the pot. Cover and simmer for 1 hour.

Add the peppercorns, bay leaves and salt and simmer for another 30 minutes.

Arrrange the vegetables in layers on top of the meat in the following order: carrots, potatoes, cauliflower, courgettes and peas. Cover and simmer gently for 1 hour.

Mix the gravy ingredients and add to the potjie. The potjie will be ready to serve after a few minutes.

Géne's special potjie

This potjie owes its delicate sweet and sour flavour to the unusual combination of wine, vinegar, Coke and honey. A pot bread is a must for mopping up the gravy. The recipe was sent in by Mr E.I. van Niekerk of Witbank. It serves 4-6 people and we recommend a no. 2 or 3 pot.

1,5 kg neck of mutton, cut into pieces	
salt to taste	
45 mℓ cooking oil	
2 medium onions, thinly sliced	
6 whole cloves	
pinch ground allspice	
pinch white pepper	
pinch dried marjoram	
250 mℓ dry white wine	
125 mℓ Coke	
100 mℓ vinegar	
30 mℓ Worcester sauce	
5 mℓ honey	
500 g whole button mushrooms	
1 small head of cabbage, cut into 6 segments	
250 mℓ whole baby carrots, peeled	
8 whole baby potatoes, peeled	
250 mℓ green beans, sliced	
250 mℓ frozen mealie kernels	
2 tomatoes, skinned and sliced	

Salt the meat. Heat the oil in the pot and brown the meat a few pieces at a time.

Remove and set aside. Fry the onions until tender. Return the meat to the pot and stir thoroughly using a wooden spoon. Add the spices and marjoram to the meat. Mix the wine, Coke, vinegar, Worcester sauce and honey and add to the meat. Stir through, replace the lid and simmer slowly for 1½ hours.

Arrange the carrots, potatoes, green beans, mealies and tomatoes in layers on top. Simmer for another hour or until the vegetables are done.

Add the mushrooms and place the cabbage on top. Simmer until the cabbage segments fall apart.

More-ish neck of mutton potjie

If you intend to entertain with this recipe, be prepared – everyone will want to know how it's made and some will even come and ask for a third helping. Ask Koos van Zyl, an ex-Brandforter now living in Magaliesburg. Serve with a pot bread. The recipe serves 6-8 people and we recommend a no. 3 pot.

60 mℓ cooking oil
4 medium onions, thinly sliced
500 g rindless streaky bacon, cut into pieces
2 kg neck of mutton, cut into pieces
salt and pepper to taste
375 mℓ water
5 mℓ dried thyme
3 mℓ dried parsley
3 mℓ lemon pepper
3 mℓ garlic salt
375 mℓ Late Harvest wine
4 large carrots, peeled and sliced
6 large potatoes, peeled and cubed
500 mℓ green beans, sliced
125 mℓ water
1 packet mushroom soup powder

Heat the oil in the pot and fry the onions until tender. Remove the onions and set aside. Fry the streaky bacon in the pot until light brown and set aside. Now fry the neck of mutton, lightly seasoned with salt and pepper, until light brown. Add the water, herbs and spices. Cover and simmer gently for approximately 45 minutes to 1 hour.

Add the wine. Arrange the vegetables in layers on top of the meat in the order as listed. Lightly salt the vegetables. Cover and simmer for 1 hour without removing the lid.

Now add the streaky bacon and onions. Mix the water and soup powder well and pour over the potjiekos. Cover and simmer for another 10 minutes. Carefully stir the potjie through once and serve.

Photo
Mixed mutton potjie
(p. 40)

Mock venison à la Koos

This recipe for mock leg of venison was sent in by Mr J.N. Cronjé of Verwoerdburg. It's a potjie that will impress the most critical of guests. Serve with a mixed salad. The recipe serves 6 people and we recommend a no. 3 pot.

2 kg leg of lamb	
250 g pork bacon, cubed	
15 mℓ ground coriander	
15 mℓ brown sugar	
1 bottle dry red wine	
30 mℓ butter	
3 mℓ dried rosemary	
250 mℓ sour cream	
150 g dried peaches	
300 g whole baby carrots	
8 medium potatoes, peeled and halved	
300 g Brussels sprouts	
salt and pepper to taste	
15 mℓ apricot jam	
15 mℓ cake flour	

Remove all superfluous fat from the leg of lamb and stuff with the pork bacon cubes. Make deep incisions in the meat, place a finger in each incision to widen it and stuff with a piece of bacon. Season the meat thoroughly with coriander and brown sugar. Marinate the leg for at least 2-3 days in wine. Turn once.

Melt the butter in the pot while the fire is still flaming and brown the leg on both sides. Add the rosemary and 50 mℓ of the wine marinade. Cover and simmer gently for 1½ hours until half-done. Check that there are not too many coals beneath the pot. Turn the leg of lamb frequently and pour some more wine and half of the sour cream over it.

Add the dried peaches, cover and simmer for 30 minutes. Arrange the vegetables in layers on top of the meat in the order as listed. Sprinkle with salt and pepper. Add the remaining sour cream and cover. Simmer for another hour.

Add the apricot jam once the leg of lamb is completely done. Replace the lid until the jam has melted. The potjie is now ready to serve.

Remove the leg of lamb and cut the meat into slices. Add the flour to the gravy and stir until done.

Photo
Sweet and sour pork potjie (p. 58)

33

Mutton shank potjie

The ideal potjie for the cook who's rushed for time – a packet of beef marinade is just about the only seasoning that's used. Be careful though not to add too much salt as the marinade is quite sharp. This tasty recipe was sent in by Hettie Lourens of Nigel. The recipe serves 4 people and we recommend a no. 2 pot.

45 mℓ cooking oil
2 kg mutton shank, cut into pieces
250 g rindless breakfast bacon, chopped
2 medium onions, chopped
salt and pepper to taste
5 bay leaves
1 packet beef marinade (prepared according to the instructions on the packet)
4 large carrots, peeled and sliced
15 whole baby potatoes, peeled
2 tomatoes, skinned and sliced
water as required

Heat the oil in the pot and fry the meat and bacon until light brown. Add the onions and fry for 10 minutes. Add the salt, pepper, bay leaves and beef marinade and fry until brown. Stir the mixture every now and then with a wooden spoon.

Arrange the carrots, potatoes and tomatoes in layers on top and cover. Simmer gently for approximately 1½ hours. Add small amounts of water as required.

Mutton potjie with a vegetable sauce

This recipe from Mr and Mrs G. van Niekerk of Wilgehof, Bloemfontein, is a delicious yet economical meal to serve guests. It is enough for 4 people, but can be stretched to fill 6 hungry stomachs if served with herbed bread or rice and a mixed salad. We recommend a no. 2 pot.

30 mℓ cooking oil
1 kg mutton shank, cut into pieces
5 mℓ salt
5 mℓ onion salt
2 medium onions, chopped
1 packet thick vegetable soup powder
500 mℓ water
500 mℓ carrots, peeled and sliced
4 medium potatoes, peeled and cubed
200 mℓ green beans, sliced

Heat the oil in the pot. Mix the salts and sprinkle over the meat. Brown the meat on both sides in the open pot. Remove and set aside. Now fry the onions until tender. Return the meat to the pot.

Dissolve the soup powder in the water and add to the meat. Cover and simmer gently for 1 hour and 15 minutes.

Arrange the carrots, potatoes and beans in layers on top of the meat. Cover and simmer for another 45 minutes.

Curry neck of mutton potjie

The recipe for this tasty curry potjie, requiring the minimum preparation, was sent to us by Mrs E.M. Cloete of Viljoensdrif. Chicken pieces can be used instead of the mutton. Serve with rice and banana slices (sprinkle with lemon juice to prevent discolouration), fresh pineapple slices and chutney. The recipe serves 4 people and we recommend a no. 2 pot.

30 mℓ cooking oil
salt and pepper to taste
1,5 kg neck of mutton, cut into slices
3 medium onions, chopped
250 mℓ water
500 g whole baby carrots, peeled
500 g whole baby potatoes, peeled
20 mℓ sugar
10 mℓ mild curry powder
5 mℓ turmeric
125 mℓ milk

Heat the oil in the pot. Season the meat with salt and pepper and brown a few pieces at a time. Remove and set aside. Fry the onions until tender. Return the meat to the pot. Cover the meat with water, replace the lid and simmer for 1 hour.

Add the carrots and potatoes and simmer for approximately 30 minutes.

Mix the sugar, curry powder and turmeric with the milk and add. Simmer for a further 15 minutes and gently stir through once.

Add more water if the potjie becomes too dry and simmer for another 15 minutes.

Mutton curry potjie

Johan and Liz Shaw of Garsfontein, Pretoria, won a third prize in *Huisgenoot's* Transvaal potjiekos competition for this delicious potjie, and a first prize in *Beeld's* potjiekos competition held on 6 April 1987. The yoghurt adds an unusual touch to the potjie. Serve with roosterkoek. The recipe serves 6-8 people and we recommend a no. 4 pot.

Marinade

30 m*l* cooking oil	
15 m*l* masala or 20 m*l* medium curry powder	
10 m*l* grated ginger root	
10 m*l* turmeric	
10 m*l* lemon juice	
5 m*l* mustard	

Meat and vegetables

2 kg mutton cubes (shank)
60 m*l* cooking oil
50 m*l* butter
4 cinnamon sticks
10 whole cloves
3 large onions, chopped
2 medium brinjals, peeled and cubed
8 whole baby potatoes, peeled
4 large, ripe tomatoes, skinned and coarsely grated
salt and pepper to taste
a little white sugar

Yoghurt mixture

500 m*l* natural yoghurt, at room temperature
20 m*l* fresh parsley, chopped
15 m*l* grated lemon peel

Mix the marinade ingredients and pour over the meat. Heat the oil and butter in the pot. Add the cinnamon and cloves and fry well. Add the onions and fry until tender. Remove the onions, but leave the cinnamon and cloves in the pot.

Brown the meat and add a little water. Return the onion mixture to the meat in the pot. Cover and simmer gently for 1 hour.

Arrange the brinjal cubes on top of the meat and season with salt and pepper. Add the potatoes and tomatoes. Sprinkle with salt and pepper to taste as well as a little sugar. Cover and simmer for 2-3 hours.

Stir the contents of the pot through gently just before serving.

Mix the yoghurt, parsley and lemon peel together. Spoon some of this mixture on top of each serving.

Hot mutton curry potjie

This potjie from Pieter Aucamp of Kuruman is for those with a weakness for strong curry. Should you prefer a weaker curry, reduce the curry powder to 15 mℓ. Serve with sliced banana, finely chopped onion, tomato and coconut. The recipe serves 6 people and we recommend a no. 3 pot.

2 kg mutton chops
salt and pepper to taste
45 mℓ cooking oil
2 large onions, coarsely chopped
250 g rindless breakfast bacon, chopped
3 large potatoes, peeled and cubed
250 mℓ uncooked rice
250 mℓ dried apricots, soaked in water for 1 hour and drained
250 mℓ water
1 tin (410 g) mealie kernels, drained
1 tin (410 g) peas, drained
250 mℓ chutney
20 mℓ strong curry powder
5 mℓ turmeric
3 mℓ coriander
3 mℓ ground nutmeg

Heat the oil in the pot. Season the meat with salt and pepper and in the open pot brown a few pieces at a time on both sides. Remove the meat and set aside. Fry the onions until tender. Return the meat to the pot with the onions. Arrange the bacon, potatoes, rice and apricots in layers on top of the meat. Add the water. Cover and simmer for 1 hour. Add more water if the potjie boils dry.

Add the mealies and peas.

Mix the chutney, curry, turmeric, coriander and nutmeg well. Add the mixture to the potjie. Cover and simmer for 30-45 minutes.

> **Hint**
> *Be careful where you put the lid when inspecting your potjie. By being careless, you could land up with grit in your potjie.*

Tripe potjie

Barry Cooke of Boksburg and his wife Priscilla were the winners of the second prize in *Huisgenoot's* Transvaal potjiekos competition. His original recipe calls for ox tripe without trotters. When testing the recipe, we used sheep's tripe and trotters. It made no difference to the taste of this delicious potjie. The recipe serves 8-10 people and we recommend a no. 4 pot.

Marinade

950 mℓ water
meat tenderiser to taste
juice of 1 lemon
1 ℓ dry white wine

2,5 kg sheep's tripe, thoroughly cleaned
500 g sheep's trotters
60 mℓ cooking oil
15 mℓ butter
6 large onions, chopped
5 cloves garlic, crushed
2 pieces fresh ginger root, crushed
1 neck of mutton, sliced
250 mℓ dry white wine
juice of 2 lemons
salt and black pepper to taste
1 tin (825 g) peach slices
12 whole baby potatoes, peeled
6 large carrots, peeled and thickly sliced
25 mℓ strong curry powder
15 mℓ chili powder
10 mℓ brown sugar
a little vinegar

Cube the tripe and marinate overnight with the trotters in the marinade.

Heat the oil and butter in the pot and fry the onions, garlic and ginger together for a few minutes until the onions are tender. Remove and set aside.

Brown the neck of mutton and add the tripe, trotters and marinade along with the wine, lemon juice, salt, pepper and the peach syrup. Cover and simmer over medium hot coals for about 3 hours until the meat mixture is tender.

Once the tripe cubes are tender and the meat comes loose from the trotters and neck vertebrae, remove the vertebrae. Simmer the meat mixture for a further 30 minutes. Then add the potatoes and carrots.

Mix the curry powder, chili powder and brown sugar with a little vinegar. Add, together with the peach slices, to the contents of the pot. Cover and simmer for a further 30 minutes. Stir the potjie thoroughly and serve.

Northern Transvaal mutton shank potjie

Here's another super recipe sent in by Colonel and Mrs D.W. van Rooyen of Garsfontein, Pretoria, which will most certainly also be enjoyed beyond the boundaries of the Northern Transvaal! Serve with rice. The recipe serves 6 people and a no. 3 pot is recommended.

2 kg mutton shank, cut into pieces
1 medium onion, finely chopped
30 mℓ cake flour
500 g potatoes, peeled and sliced
300 g whole, young green beans
300 g whole button mushrooms
200 g butternut, sliced

Marinade

750 mℓ dry white wine
250 mℓ beef stock
10 mℓ dried oregano
10 mℓ dried rosemary
10 mℓ salt
5 mℓ grated orange peel
2 mℓ pepper

Heat the pot. Place the meat in the pot and cover. Steam for approximately 45 minutes. Add the onion and fry gently for 15 minutes. Sprinkle the flour over the meat and stir thoroughly to thicken the gravy.

Arrange the potatoes, green beans, mushrooms and butternut in layers on top of the meat. Add the marinade. Simmer the potjie for approximately another 1½ hours.

Hint
A little grated orange peel in your marinade adds real magic.

39

Leg of lamb potjie

Hint

Lemon juice is inclined to toughen vegetables.

The recipe for this hearty potjie was sent in by Mr H.J. van Aswegen of Krugersdorp North. It's a good substitute for the traditional Sunday leg of mutton. Serve with a pot bread or rice and a mixed salad. The recipe serves 4-6 people and we recommend a no. 2 or 3 pot.

1 kg leg of mutton, cut into 3 cm cubes
15 mℓ butter
3 medium onions, sliced
7 whole baby potatoes, peeled
5 whole baby carrots, peeled
6 whole courgettes
250 mℓ meat stock
2,5 mℓ salt
1,2 mℓ celery salt
30 mℓ Worcester sauce
10 mℓ soy sauce
10 mℓ lemon juice
1,2 mℓ dried thyme
15 mℓ brown gravy powder (e.g. Bisto)
15 mℓ mushroom soup powder

Heat the butter in the pot. Stir fry the onions until tender. Move the onions to one side and place the meat next to the onions in the pot. Using a large spoon, place the onions on top of the meat. Cover and cook the meat for about 30 minutes or until it renders its own juice.

Place the potatoes on top of the meat without letting them touch the sides of the pot. Arrange the carrots in a circle around the potatoes and place the courgettes on top. Mix 125 mℓ of the stock with the salt, celery salt, Worcester sauce, soy sauce, lemon juice and thyme, and add to the pot. Cover and simmer for about 1½ hours.

Use the remaining 125 mℓ meat stock mixed with the gravy powder and soup powder to thicken the gravy. Pour over the potjie and simmer thoroughly for about 10 minutes.

Mixed mutton potjie

This recipe, sent in by Martie van Aswegen of Bainsvlei in the Free State, is perfect for special guests, yet quick and easy to prepare, especially when using frozen vegetables. Serve with yellow rice and raisins or a pot bread.

Chicken portions can be used instead of the mutton. You'll also find that any leftovers taste even better the following day. The recipe serves 6-8 people and we recommend a no. 3 pot.

butter or oil
2 kg mutton, including shanks, neck and ribs, cut into portions
2 medium onions, finely chopped
20 whole baby potatoes, peeled
10 whole baby carrots, peeled (or 1 kg frozen mixed vegetables. Add after 1 ¾ hours)
3 medium sweet potatoes, peeled and sliced
salt to taste

Gravy

500 mℓ warm water
2 beef stock cubes
250 mℓ dry red wine
50 mℓ chutney
50 mℓ tomato sauce
50 mℓ Worcester sauce
30 mℓ cornflour
30 mℓ oxtail soup powder
25 mℓ soy sauce
15 mℓ brown gravy powder (e.g. Bisto)
10 mℓ garlic flakes
0,6 mℓ ground cloves

Grease the pot well with butter or oil and heat until very hot. Brown the meat a few pieces at a time. Remove and set aside. The meat will now have rendered its own fat. Fry the onions in the meat fat until tender. Return the meat to the pot and arrange evenly.

Dissolve the stock cubes in the warm water and mix the remaining gravy ingredients with the water and wine. Pour the gravy over the potjie and add salt to taste.

Arrrange the potatoes, carrots and sweet potatoes in layers on top of the meat. Cover and simmer for approximately 2½ hours.

Vaatjie's neck of mutton potjie

Mr H.F. Coetzee of Virginia's friends can vouch for the virtues of this potjie. The noodles and vegetables make it a filling meal which does not call for any side dishes. The recipe serves 6 people and we recommend a no. 2 pot.

1,5 kg neck of mutton, cut into pieces
125 mℓ cake flour
125 mℓ cooking oil
4 medium onions, chopped
625 mℓ port
1 ℓ water
250 mℓ uncooked shell noodles
1 green pepper, seeded and finely chopped
8 carrots, peeled and quite thickly sliced
8 medium potatoes, peeled and cubed
8 whole courgettes
300 g fresh button mushrooms
15 mℓ salt
15 mℓ freshly scorched, ground coriander
5 mℓ dry mixed herbs
3 whole cloves
7 black peppercorns
1,5 mℓ ground nutmeg

Coat the meat with flour. Heat the oil in the pot and brown the meat. Add the onions and braise with the meat in the open pot. Add 125 mℓ port and 125 mℓ water. Cover and simmer gently for 45 minutes.

Sprinkle the noodles and pepper on top of the meat. Arrange the vegetables in layers in the following order: carrots, potatoes, courgettes and mushrooms. Add the salt, herbs and spices as well as 500 mℓ port and the remaining water. Cover and simmer for 2½ hours. Do not remove the lid.

Mutton potjie with port

All the good things in life take time – so prepare yourself for a long cosy evening round the fire when serving this potjie. A pot bread is the perfect side dish and for a bit of variety, substitute the shoulder of mutton for a shoulder of venison, in which case you should add 30-45 minutes to the cooking time.

This recipe was sent in by Rita Eloff of Wilgehof, Bloemfontein. It serves 6 people and we recommend a no. 2 pot.

125 g butter
45 mℓ cooking oil
4 carrots, peeled and cubed
2 medium onions, sliced
4 cloves garlic, crushed and finely chopped
4 sprigs fresh thyme
1 bay leaf
1 shoulder of mutton, cut into 2,5 cm cubes
250 g pork bacon, cubed
salt and pepper to taste
½ bottle port
6 medium potatoes, peeled and cubed

Heat the pot and add the butter and oil. Once the butter has melted, add the carrots, onions, garlic, thyme and bay leaf. Place the meat and bacon on top and sprinkle with salt and pepper. Pour the port over the meat, cover and gently simmer for 3 hours.

Place the potatoes on top of the meat and simmer for another hour. By this time, your potjie should have a rich, thick gravy. If the gravy is too thin, mash a few of the potatoes and stir through.

43

Calvinia's North-Western potjie

Cobus Hough of Calvinia sent in this mouthwatering recipe. He says that potjiekos was the staple diet of the cattle farmers in the North-West when they trekked with their cattle in search of grazing. Their potjie usually consisted of only meat with a piece of dough on top. However, they added vegetables when these were available. To complete the meal, they served pot bread with goat's butter and wild honey. The recipe serves 4-6 people and we recommend a no. 3 pot.

45 ml cooking oil
3 medium onions, sliced
1,5 kg mutton chine, cut into pieces
375 ml dry white wine
6 medium carrots, peeled and sliced into strips
6 medium potatoes, peeled and sliced
500 g green beans, sliced
250 g whole button mushrooms
10 dried peaches, soaked in water for 1 hour
salt and pepper to taste
125 ml water
1 packet mushroom soup powder

Heat the oil in the pot and fry the onions until tender. Place the meat on top and season with salt and pepper to taste. Add a little wine. Cover and simmer gently for 45 minutes. Stir the meat and onions through once.

Arrange the carrots, potatoes and green beens in layers on top of the meat. Sprinkle with a little salt and pepper and add a little wine. Replace the lid and simmer for another hour.

Arrange the mushrooms and peaches on top and sprinkle with some more salt. Add the remaining wine. Cover and simmer for 30 minutes. Mix the water and soup powder and add the mixture to the potjie. Cover and simmer for another 15 minutes. This potjie should at all times be cooked over a very low heat.

Oukraal potjie

This divine potjie has already won three prizes – a first prize at a competition in Bellville and at the Wellington Autumn Festival, plus a second prize at the Boland Show. Thank you, Mrs A.M. Rossouw of Paarl, for sharing your recipe with us.

Mrs Rossouw says that if one arranges the potjie in concentric circles instead of layers, one can immediately see all the ingredients, making it easier to serve. The recipe serves 6 people and we recommend a no. 3 pot.

30 mℓ butter or Holsum fat	
1 oxtail, cut into joints	
500 g mutton shank, cut into pieces	
500 g sheep's tail or mutton ribs	
8 medium onions, chopped	
250 g breakfast bacon, chopped	
4 beef stock cubes, crumbed	
10 pimento corns	
8 whole cloves	
4 cloves garlic, chopped	
10 mℓ dried mixed herbs	
1 cinnamon stick	
1 red chili	
freshly ground pepper to taste	
125 mℓ dry red wine	
62 mℓ water	
500 mℓ green beans, sliced	
1 bunch whole baby carrots, peeled	
½ small head of cauliflower, broken into florets	
300 g whole button mushrooms	
1 green pepper, coarsely chopped	
15 whole baby potatoes, peeled	
2 celery sticks, chopped	
15 whole button onions	
grated nutmeg to taste	
15 g brown onion soup powder	
coarsely chopped parsley	

Heat the butter or fat in the potjie. Fry the meat for 15 minutes until brown. Add the onions, bacon, beef stock, spices and herbs (excluding the parsley and nutmeg) and fry for another 15 minutes. Remove the mutton and set aside.

Add the wine and water to the oxtail. Cover and simmer for 1 hour. Return the mutton to the pot and simmer for 50 minutes.

Arrange the vegetables as follows: a ring of green beans along the inside of the pot, carrots on the inside of this ring, and the cauliflower right in the centre. Pack the mushrooms tightly along the inside of the pot between the green beans and sprinkle the green pepper on top. Pack the potatoes in between the beans and carrots and sprinkle with the celery. Arrange the onions around the cauliflower. Sprinkle the cauliflower with nutmeg and then sprinkle the soup powder and parsley on top. Cover and simmer gently for another 2 hours until the vegetables are tender.

Do not use any salt – the soup powder and beef stock make the potjie salty enough.

Hint
Some people prefer a combination of meats, for example, shank of mutton and beef short-rib. Remember, however, to place the meat that takes the longest to cook in the pot first.

45

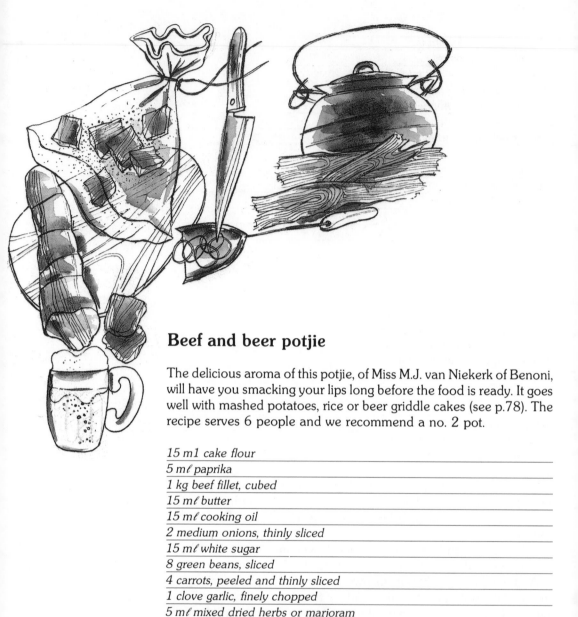

Beef and beer potjie

The delicious aroma of this potjie, of Miss M.J. van Niekerk of Benoni, will have you smacking your lips long before the food is ready. It goes well with mashed potatoes, rice or beer griddle cakes (see p.78). The recipe serves 6 people and we recommend a no. 2 pot.

15 mℓ cake flour
5 mℓ paprika
1 kg beef fillet, cubed
15 mℓ butter
15 mℓ cooking oil
2 medium onions, thinly sliced
15 mℓ white sugar
8 green beans, sliced
4 carrots, peeled and thinly sliced
1 clove garlic, finely chopped
5 mℓ mixed dried herbs or marjoram
375 mℓ beer
250 mℓ beef stock
1 packet tomato soup powder
1 bay leaf
15 mℓ vinegar
10 mℓ cornflour
salt and pepper to taste

Combine the paprika and flour and place in a plastic bag. Add the meat cubes and shake well to coat the meat. Melt the butter and oil in the pot and brown the meat over medium hot coals. Remove and set aside.

Fry the onions and sugar, stirring now and then until the onions are tender. Add the beans, carrots and garlic, cover and simmer for 5 minutes.

Return the meat to the pot and stir in the herbs, beer, stock, soup powder and bay leaf. Replace the lid and simmer until the meat is tender, approximately 45 minutes to 1 hour. Stir occasionally, using a wooden spoon.

Mix the vinegar and cornflour and stir in. Simmer until the gravy has thickened and season with salt and pepper.

Beef potjie

In order to enjoy every drop of the delicious gravy, you simply have to serve mashed potatoes or a pot bread with this potjie of Mr and Mrs I.B. Vorster of Boshof. Green peas with a knob of butter is also a good accompaniment. The recipe serves 6 people and we recommend a no. 2 pot.

200 mℓ cake flour
2 kg beef, cubed
60 mℓ cooking oil
15 mℓ butter
2 large onions, finely chopped
4 whole cloves
salt and pepper to taste
250 mℓ water
30 mℓ tomato paste
250 mℓ semi-dry white wine
1 tin (285 g) cream of mushroom soup
250 mℓ sour cream

Place the flour in a plastic bag, add the meat and shake until the meat is well coated with the flour. Heat the oil and butter in the pot and fry the meat briefly, taking care that the pot does not become too hot and burn the meat. Add the onions and fry until tender. Add the cloves, salt and pepper. Mix the water, tomato paste and wine, and add. Cover and simmer for 2 hours. Stir occasionally.

Once the meat is tender, add the soup. Cover and simmer for another 30 minutes.

Add the sour cream and simmer only 10 minutes longer.

Hint
If your gravy tends to be too thin, thicken it with ingredients like Bisto or cake flour. However, do not simply stir it in. Rather pour it in carefully against the side of the potjie, tipping the potjie to the left and the right in semicircles. This method is most successful.

Oxtail and banana potjie

This hearty potjie is perfect for cold winter evenings – only, your family will want it throughout the year! Kobus Rossouw of Northern Paarl sent in this recipe. Serve with brown or white rice. The recipe serves 5-6 people and we recommend a no. 2 or 3 pot.

30 mℓ butter or margarine
1 large oxtail, cut into joints
3 medium onions, thinly sliced
2 cloves garlic, finely chopped
½ red chilli, finely chopped, or 1,2 mℓ chili powder
5 whole cloves
5 mℓ dried mixed herbs
2 bay leaves
salt and pepper to taste
500 mℓ warm water
2 ripe bananas, sliced
5 medium carrots, peeled and sliced into strips
12 whole baby potatoes, peeled
250 g whole button mushrooms
1 large tomato, skinned and sliced
5 mℓ chopped parsley
10 whole button onions

Sauce

62 mℓ brown vinegar
20 mℓ tomato sauce
20 mℓ chutney
20 mℓ honey
10 mℓ mild curry powder

Heat the butter or margarine in the pot and fry the meat for 15 minutes. Add the onions, garlic, chili, cloves, herbs, bay leaves and salt and pepper to taste. Fry for another 15 minutes. Should the potjie become too dry, add a little hot water. Add 500 mℓ hot water. Cover and simmer the meat gently for 2 hours.

In the meantime, mix the gravy ingredients and set aside.

Arrange the banana on top of the meat. Arrange the vegetables on top of this in the order as listed. Sprinkle the parsley on top. Arrange the onions at the very top and simmer for 1 hour.

Add the gravy and simmer for a further 30 minutes.

Photo
Beef and beer potjie
(p. 46)

Beef and vegetable potjie

Mr N.E. Smuts of Fleurdal, Bloemfontein, sent us the recipe for this tasty potjie with its delicious assortment of vegetables. Serve your favourite salad as a side dish. Do not add any extra salt as the soy sauce is salty enough. Port can be used instead of sherry. The recipe serves 6 people and we recommend a no. 2 pot.

Gravy
125 mℓ sweet sherry
125 mℓ soy sauce
5 mℓ black pepper
3 mℓ dry mustard
1 mℓ dried rosemary
1 mℓ dried thyme
1 beef stock cube
500 mℓ boiling water

30 mℓ cooking oil
1 ox kidney, cubed
1 kg stewing beef, cubed
2 medium onions, sliced
125 mℓ dried apricots or peaches, soaked in water for 1 hour and drained
4 carrots, peeled and sliced
2 sweet potatoes, peeled and sliced
4 medium potatoes, peeled and halved
6 courgettes, sliced
250 mℓ cabbage, shredded
1 tomato, skinned and sliced
black pepper to taste
30 mℓ dried parsley

Heat the oil in the pot. Fry the meat and ox kidney until nearly brown. Add the onions and brown.

Mix all the ingredients for the gravy with the boiling water and add to the meat. Stir well, using a wooden spoon. Cover and simmer gently for 1½ hours.

Now arrange first the dried fruit and then the vegetables on the meat in the order as listed. Sprinkle the tomato with a little black pepper. Sprinkle the parsley on top and cover. Simmer the potjie for another 2 hours until the vegetables are done.

Photo
Beef and vegetable potjie

Spicy curry potjie

You'll find that it's not only the curry lovers who'll tuck into this delicious potjie of Mrs B. Botha of Silverton, Pretoria. The recipe serves a large number of guests (10-12) using a no. 6 pot. However, if there are fewer mouths to feed, halve the recipe and use a no. 3 pot. The cooking time will also be shorter then. Serve with a tomato and onion salad as well as sliced bananas.

Stock

2 beef shank bones
2 carrots, peeled
3 onions
6 black peppercorns
15 mℓ brown vinegar
7,5 mℓ brown sugar
± 1,5 ℓ water

15 mℓ pork fat
2 kg beef shank, carved into slices
1 kg ox kidney, sliced into large flat rounds
6 large onions, sliced
8 cloves garlic, chopped very finely
3 green peppers, cut into strips
800 mℓ water
1 packet black pepper sauce
50 mℓ brown gravy powder (e.g. Bisto)
40 mℓ turmeric
20 mℓ ground ginger
20 mℓ mild curry powder
15 mℓ brown sugar
750 g green beans, sliced
30 whole baby carrots, peeled
30 whole baby potatoes, peeled
salt to taste

Prepare the stock in advance.

Heat the pork fat in the pot. Brown the meat and kidney lightly. Add the onions and garlic to the meat and fry for 20 minutes. Add the green pepper and 1,5 ℓ stock, cover and simmer for 2 hours.

Mix all the seasonings with 800 mℓ water. Arrange the vegetables in layers on top of the meat in the order as listed and pour the seasoned water on top. Add salt to taste. Replace the lid and simmer slowly for 2 hours or until the meat is tender and the vegetables are done. Add more water if necessary.

Garlic and oxtail potjie

This recipe for oxtail potjie, sent in by Mr C.L. Pieterse of Riebeeckstad, is a real winner. Pearl wheat goes well with the thick, tasty gravy. The recipe serves 4 people and we recommend a no. 2 pot.

1,5 kg oxtail, cut into joints
1 packet garlic steak marinade, prepared with water according to the instructions on the packet
30 mℓ olive oil
2 medium onions, sliced
250 mℓ red wine
salt and pepper to taste
250 g whole baby carrots, peeled
3 medium potatoes, peeled and sliced
250 g frozen green peas
300 g mushrooms, sliced
1 tin (405 g) cream of mushroom soup

Marinate the oxtail in the garlic marinade for 1 hour, turning the meat every now and then.

Heat the oil in the pot, add the meat and onions, cover and simmer for approximately 45 minutes.

Mix the red wine with the marinade and add. Cover and simmer for another 3 hours or until the meat is tender. Add a little water if the meat becomes too dry.

Season with salt and pepper. Arrange the carrots, potatoes and peas in layers on top of the meat. Cover and simmer for a further 45 minutes.

Add the mushrooms and soup, cover and simmer for 30 minutes.

Green mealies and oxtail potjie

Hint

A piece of smoked ham or Russian sausages add real flavour to beef and chicken.

This potjie, created by Tienie Ferreira of Secunda in the Transvaal, is finger-licking good – both the green mealies and juicy bones taste best when eaten with the fingers. Pearl wheat makes an excellent side dish. The recipe serves 6 people and we recommend a no. 3 pot.

30 mℓ cooking oil
1 oxtail, cut into joints
2 onions, sliced
1 green pepper, seeded and chopped
5 black peppercorns
3 bay leaves
1 ℓ hot water
1 packet brown onion soup powder
1 tin (115 g) tomato paste
250 mℓ water
4 carrots, peeled and sliced
5 medium potatoes, peeled and halved
250 g green beans, sliced
150 g Brussels sprouts
6 whole yellow or green gem squashes
4 green mealies, cut into portions
salt and pepper to taste
15 mℓ chopped parsley

Heat the oil in the pot. Brown the meat slightly, remove and set aside. Fry the onions and pepper until tender. Add the pepper corns and bay leaves and return the meat to the pot. Cover with hot water, replace the lid and simmer for approximately 2¼ hours.

Mix the soup powder and tomato paste with 250 mℓ water and add to the meat. Arrange the vegetables in layers in the order as listed and sprinkle with salt and pepper. Replace the lid and simmer very gently for about 1 hour until the vegetables are tender and the mealies at the top are done. The gravy is very thick and will burn easily – so do not lift the lid unnecessarily. However, take a peek every now and then just to check – replenish the potjie with water if it becomes too dry.

Sprinkle with parsley just before serving.

Oxtail potjie

The recipe for this flavoursome potjie was sent in by Marita Botha of Middelburg in the Cape. Stewed dried fruit or baked sweet potatoes is a perfect side dish. The recipe serves 4 people and we recommend a no. 2 pot.

1 kg oxtail, cut into joints
500 ml water
300 ml red wine
6-8 whole button onions, peeled
375 ml whole baby carrots, peeled
8 whole baby potatoes, peeled
375 ml frozen green peas
250 ml water
25 g oxtail soup powder
5 ml salt
5 ml ground allspice

Heat the pot until very hot. Brown the meat in its own fat. Add the water and the wine, cover and simmer gently for 1 hour.

Add the onions, replace the lid and simmer for another 2 hours. Have an occasional peek, adding more water if necessary.

Arrange the carrots, potatoes and peas in layers on top of the meat. Cover and simmer for another hour.

Mix the water, soup powder, salt and allspice and add. Simmer for 15 minutes.

Boland potjie

A helping of this filling potjie from Bettie van Tonder of Monte Vista in the Cape is a meal worth waiting for. As a final touch, sprinkle some dried thyme over the potjie just before serving. The recipe serves 8 people and we recommend a no. 3 pot.

10 dried peaches, sliced
10 dried pears, sliced
6 dried apple rings
60 mℓ sherry
15 mℓ cooking oil
15 mℓ butter
1,5 kg lean stewing lamb, cubed
300 g lean stewing beef, cubed
salt and pepper to taste
3 large onions, sliced
1 clove garlic, finely chopped
2 large tomatoes, skinned and chopped
250 mℓ dry white wine
5 mℓ brown sugar
2 bay leaves
6 large carrots, peeled and sliced
250 mℓ uncooked rice
500 mℓ green beans, sliced
2 mℓ prepared French mustard
2,5 mℓ lemon pepper
6 medium potatoes, peeled and cubed
500 mℓ boiling water
4 mℓ ground coriander

Marinate the dried fruit in the sherry for 1 hour.

Heat the oil and butter in the pot. Season the meat with salt and pepper and brown lightly. Add the onions and garlic and fry for approximately 15 minutes. Add the tomatoes and 125 mℓ of the wine. Place a layer of the marinated dried fruit on top of the tomatoes. Sprinkle with sugar and add the bay leaves. Arrange the carrots on top and add the rest of the dried fruit. Sprinkle the rice on top and then the green beans.

Mix the remaining 125 mℓ wine with the mustard and lemon pepper and pour on top. Add salt to taste. Arrange the potatoes on top. Add boiling water and sprinkle with the coriander. Cover and simmer gently for 2½-3 hours. Watch the potjie closely – add boiling water if it becomes too dry, but replace the lid immediately.

Old-fashioned meat and vegetable potjie

If you've had enough of complicated recipes and you feel like some straightforward "boerekos", this tasty potjie of Ockert van Zyl of Fichardtpark, Bloemfontein, is just up your street. It goes well with a pot bread or a date pot pudding (see p.79) for afters. The recipe serves 6 people and we recommend a no. 3 pot.

45 mℓ cooking oil
2 onions, chopped
2 kg beef shank, carved in pieces
salt to taste
500 mℓ water
8 medium carrots, peeled and halved
8 medium potatoes, peeled and halved
250 mℓ green beans, sliced
8 courgettes, sliced
250 mℓ Brussels sprouts
200 g whole button mushrooms
2 tomatoes, skinned and sliced
lemon pepper to taste

Heat the oil in the pot and fry the onions until tender. Add the meat and season with salt. Add 250 mℓ of the water. Cover and simmer over medium hot coals for approximately 2 hours. Stir the meat now and then. Add the remaining water as required.

Arrange the vegetables in layers on top of the meat in the order as listed. Add lemon pepper. Cover and simmer for approximately another 1 hour. Do not stir again.

Beef and pork potjie

Once you've had a taste of this delicious, colourful potjie of Adam and Anna Dunn of Bellville, you'll understand why they walked off with the first prize in *Huisgenoot's* Cape potjiekos competition. Arrange the dumplings amongst the vegetables and not on top. The recipe serves 6 people and we recommend a no. 3 pot.

1 kg stewing beef, cubed
500 g pork, cubed
juice of 4-5 lemons
cooking oil
2 large onions, chopped
2 beef stock cubes, crumbled
50 mℓ tomato sauce
25 mℓ soy sauce
1 large clove garlic, crushed
1 tin (410 g) whole tomatoes (2 tomatoes and the juice are used)
375 mℓ dry white wine
sugar to taste
8 whole baby potatoes, peeled
8 whole baby carrots, peeled
5 button onions
4 pieces butternut
8 florets fresh/frozen broccoli
salt to taste

Dumplings

125 mℓ cake flour
5 mℓ baking powder
pinch salt
5 mℓ butter or margarine
1 egg, beaten

Marinate the meat cubes for 3 hours in the lemon juice. Heat a little oil in the pot and brown the meat. Remove and set aside. Fry the onions until tender. Return the meat to the pot and add the marinade juices, beef stock, tomato and soy sauce, garlic, the juice of the tin of tomatoes and the white wine. Cover and simmer for 1-1½ hours. Add sugar.

To make the dumplings, sift the flour, baking powder and salt together. Rub in the butter or margarine. Add the egg and mix well. Spoon large teaspoonfuls of the dough into the pot.

Arrange the vegetables in the following order, taking care not to cover the dumplings completely: place the potatoes in the centre and the carrots and small onions along the inside of the pot. Place pieces of butternut and broccoli amongst the potatoes and carrots. Sprinkle with a little salt and replace the lid. Simmer for approximately 1 hour.

Pork fillet potjie

Who said potjiekos is not up to gourmet standards? Miemie Louw from De Tuin, De Hoek, in the Cape and her team mate, Ester Wege, won a third prize in *Huisgenoot's* Cape potjiekos competition with this unusual recipe. Served with their "potballetjies" (see p.71), it's a real winner. The recipe serves 6-8 people and we recommend a no. 4 pot.

2 pork fillets of approximately 700 g each
20 large stoned prunes
10 smoked oysters
20 mℓ butter
20 mℓ cooking oil
15 mℓ cake flour
250-300 mℓ meat stock
125 mℓ red wine
salt to taste
5 mℓ black pepper
12 whole button onions
5 celery sticks, cut into strips
12 whole baby potatoes, peeled
5 mℓ cornflour
freshly chopped parsley for garnishing

Slit each fillet lengthwise and open carefully. Stuff 10 prunes with an oyster each. Arrange the stuffed prunes lengthwise on one of the splayed-out fillets and place the second fillet on top. Fasten the fillets tightly with string.

Brown the meat in the butter and oil until brown. Sprinkle with flour and fry for a further 2 minutes. Add the stock and the wine, stirring the gravy with a wooden spoon until smooth. Season the meat with salt and black pepper, replace the lid and simmer the potjie gently for 1 hour.

Remove the string carefully, slice the meat and pack the slices together again.

Arrange the vegetables around the meat in the pot. Add the remaining prunes and a little of the stock if necessary and simmer until the vegetables are done.

Thicken the gravy with the cornflour mixed with water, if necessary. Sprinkle with fresh parsley and serve.

> **Hint**
> *Cut meat (and vegetables) into bite-size pieces. Your guests should not even require a knife.*

57

Otjie-potjie

You'd go far to find a potjie with a wider variety of vegetables than this great pork potjie of Tienie Ferreira who hails from Secunda. The recipe serves 6 people and we recommend a no. 3 pot.

30 mℓ olive oil
1,5 kg pork shank, cut into pieces
salt and pepper to taste
250 g rindless breakfast bacon, chopped
1 large onion, sliced
1 green pepper, sliced into rings
1 clove garlic, chopped
1 tin (115 g) tomato paste
100 mℓ water
6 medium potatoes, peeled and cubed
4 carrots, peeled and sliced
3 celery sticks, chopped
2 turnips, peeled and chopped
1 leek, sliced (use white part only)
500 mℓ green beans, sliced
500 mℓ cabbage, shredded
2,5 mℓ mixed spice

Heat the oil in the pot. Sprinkle the shank with salt and pepper and brown slightly. Remove and set aside. Sauté the bacon, onion, green pepper and garlic for 15 minutes in the oil. Return the meat to the pot. Mix the tomato paste with the water and pour over the meat. Cover and simmer gently for 30 minutes. Arrange the vegetables in layers on top of the meat in the order as listed. Sprinkle with mixed spice, replace the lid again and simmer for 1 hour until the vegetables are done.

Sweet and sour pork potjie

Wrong, this isn't our first potjiekos recipe from China – it was sent in by Mrs M.S. Steenkamp of Hotazel in the Cape. Serve this unusual dish with rice or any kind of noodles. The recipe serves 6 people and we recommend a no. 2 pot.

15 mℓ margarine or butter	
2 large onions, sliced	
1 green pepper, cut into strips	
2 kg leg of pork, cubed	
10 mℓ mixed spice	
salt and pepper to taste	
1 large pineapple, peeled and cubed	
1 large cooking apple, peeled and cubed	
125 mℓ brown vinegar	
60 mℓ cornflour	
60 mℓ brown sugar	
60 mℓ red wine	
25 mℓ Worcester sauce	
250 mℓ boiling water	

Melt the butter or margarine in the pot and fry the onions and green pepper until tender. Remove and set aside. Brown the meat cubes, and sprinkle with spices, salt and pepper. Place the pineapple on top of the meat, then the apple and finally the onion and green pepper mixture. Combine the vinegar, cornflour, sugar, wine, Worcester sauce and boiling water and pour over the mixture. Replace the lid and simmer gently for approximately 2 hours.

Seafood potjies

Paella potjie

This delicious paella recipe was sent in by Colonel D.W. van Rooyen from Garsfontein, Pretoria and we predict it will be a real winner. Serve with a mixed salad. The recipe serves 6 people, including a second helping for each, and we recommend a no. 3 pot.

60 mℓ cooking oil
3 red sweet peppers, seeded and cut in strips (or a 400 g tin pimento)
1 large onion, chopped
500 g pork, cubed
5 chicken thighs, halved
1 ℓ boiling water
5 mℓ saffron
4 bay leaves
2 chicken stock cubes
1 kg kingklip fillets, cut in strips
400 g frozen prawns
500 g uncooked rice
salt and pepper to taste
250 g frozen green peas
juice of 1 lemon

Heat the oil in the pot. Lightly brown the pepper, onion, pork and chicken. Cover and simmer slowly for 1 hour or until the meat is nearly done.

Add the saffron, bay leaves and chicken stock cubes to the boiling water and set aside.

Place the fish and prawns on top of the meat, followed by the rice and peas. Season with salt and pepper to taste. Add the saffron water little by little as the rice boils dry. Simmer the potjie gently until the rice and peas are done and all the liquid has nearly boiled away. Paella should be loose and the rice should not be soggy.

Add the lemon juice just before serving and stir well.

Crayfish potjie

If you've always liked crayfish cooked on its own, try it with the tasty rice in this potjie recipe sent in by Gerhard Fritz and Koos Myburgh from Helderberg in the Cape. Take care not to simmer the potjie too rapidly as the rice burns easily. The recipe serves 6 people, but if extra guests arrive unexpectedly, simply add a few pieces of kingklip fillets. We recommend a no. 3 pot.

45 mℓ cooking oil
750 mℓ uncooked rice
1 medium onion, chopped
1 green pepper
1,5 ℓ water
10 mℓ dried parsley
juice of 1 lemon
150 g fresh mushrooms, sliced
2 tomatoes, skinned and peeled
1 packet thick white onion soup powder
10 mℓ garlic salt
6 uncooked medium crayfish tails
salt to taste

Heat the oil in the pot and fry the rice for a few minutes. Add the onion and pepper and fry till tender. Soak the parsley in the water for 15 minutes. Add the parsley water and the remaining ingredients, except the crayfish, to the potjie. Sprinkle with salt, cover and simmer gently for 30 minutes or until the rice is nearly done.

Place the crayfish on top and simmer gently for 15 minutes. Do not cook the crayfish for much longer as it may become floury.

Remove the crayfish and shell. Serve on top of the rice mixture, accompanied by a green salad.

Perlemoen potjie

This unusual recipe from Braam Rust of Durbanville is bound to attract a large following. It truly does justice to the delicate taste of the perlemoen. Serve on rice and add a few extra drops of lemon juice. The recipe serves 4-5 people and we recommend a no. 2 pot.

250 g butter
5 medium perlemoen, beaten until the muscle has loosened
2 onions, finely chopped
2 carrots, peeled and sliced
2 tomatoes, peeled and chopped
1 green pepper, seeded and finely chopped
juice of 1 lemon
125 mℓ dry white wine
5 mℓ salt
5 mℓ freshly ground black pepper
1,2 mℓ grated nutmeg
125 mℓ fresh cream

Heat the potjie and melt 50 g butter in it. Add the perlemoen, cover and steam for 20 minutes. Remove the perlemoen and cut into small cubes. Reserve the juice in the pot.

Fry the onions for a few minutes in the juice. Return the perlemoen to the pot and arrange the carrots, tomatoes and green pepper in layers on top. Mix the lemon juice and white wine and pour over the potjie. Add the salt and pepper. Sprinkle with the nutmeg. Add the remaining 200 g butter and simmer for 1 hour. Add the cream and simmer gently for 30 minutes.

Seafood potjie

If you enjoy seafood, this novel potjie from Mrs M.C. Cillié of Stellenbosch will be a real treat. Serve it with a steamed milk bread (see p.75) or pot bread. As a starter it serves 6 and as a main course 4 people. We recommend a no. 3 pot.

50 black mussels

125 mℓ dry white wine

45 mℓ butter

2 cloves garlic, finely chopped

250 mℓ parsley, finely chopped

1 large onion, finely chopped

1 tomato, skinned and chopped

pinch dried thyme

freshly ground black pepper to taste

juice of 1 lemon

1 cooked crayfish or 6 prawns

250 mℓ fresh cream

Scrape all growths from the mussel shells and soak the mussels in sea or salt water to open them up. Remove the beard and rinse mussels in fresh water.

Add the wine, butter, garlic, parsley, onion, tomato, thyme, pepper and the mussels to the pot, cover and simmer slowly for approximately 15 minutes. Sprinkle with lemon juice and add the crayfish or prawns. Simmer for a further 10 minutes and add the cream.

Soup potjies

Hotch-potch bean soup potjie

Here's a wonderfully hearty soup recipe, sent in by Denise Loeblich of Camps Bay. We recommend a no. 2 pot.

500 g dried beans
3-4 ℓ water
6 slices mutton shank
4 slices beef shank
1 beef stock cube, crumbled
1,5 mℓ fresh parsley, chopped
5 mℓ garlic flakes
5 mℓ dried oregano
3 bay leaves
4 medium carrots, peeled and sliced
2 medium onions, finely chopped
2 large potatoes, peeled and cubed
2 celery sticks, chopped
2 large tomatoes, skinned and chopped
salt and pepper to taste

Wash the beans and soak overnight in cold water. Drain and place the beans in the pot, adding 3 ℓ water. Cover and simmer gently for 2 hours. Add the meat and stock cube, cover and simmer for a further 30 minutes. Stir occasionally.

Add the remaining ingredients and season with salt and pepper and cover. Stir the soup through and cover. Simmer for another 1½ hours. Should the soup be too thick, dilute with the remaining water.

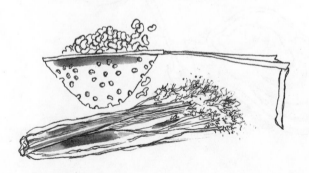

Photo
Paella potjie (p. 60)

Pea soup potjie

This recipe for pea soup, sent in by Jeanne Hammann of Llandudno in the Cape, is a real standby. We recommend a no. 3 pot.

800 g neck of mutton, sliced
1 small, whole pork shank
5 ℓ water
100 mℓ celery sticks, finely chopped
4 strips rindless breakfast bacon, cut into strips
2 large potatoes, peeled and coarsely grated
2 large carrots, peeled and coarsely grated
1 large onion, finely chopped
2 bay leaves
500 g dried split peas
125 mℓ uncooked rice
salt and pepper to taste

Place all the ingredients, excepting the peas and rice, along with 2 ℓ water in the pot. Cover and bring to the boil. Lower the heat and simmer the potjie slowly for approximately 2 hours.

Add the peas, rice, 2,5 ℓ water and salt and pepper. Cover and simmer for 1½-2 hours. If the soup is very thick, add the remaining 500 mℓ water, or more. Stir frequently to prevent the soup from burning.

Photo
Crayfish potjie (p. 61)

65

Tomato and barley soup potjie

The recipe for this flavoursome soup potjie was sent in by Jeanne Hammann of Llandudno in the Cape. We recommend a no. 3 pot.

4 slices beef shank
6 slices neck of mutton
6 whole cloves
3 large carrots, peeled and coarsely grated
2 large onions, chopped
4-5 ℓ water
300 g pearl barley
3 tins (115 g each) tomato paste
salt and pepper to taste

Place all the ingredients, excepting the barley and tomato paste, along with 2 ℓ water in the pot. Cover and bring to the boil. Reduce the heat and simmer for 2 hours.

Add the barley, tomato paste, 2,5 ℓ water and salt and pepper. Cover and simmer for 1½ hours. If the soup is too thick, add the remaining water. Stir frequently to prevent the soup from burning.

Chicken soup potjie

The only meal to equal a potjie on a cold winter's evening is a soup potjie. This delicious recipe for chicken soup potjie was sent in by Denise Loeblich of Camps Bay. We recommend a no. 2 pot.

1 braai pack chicken
3,5 ℓ water
5 mℓ chicken stock powder
5 mℓ dried parsley
5 mℓ tarragon
3 bay leaves
2 medium onions, finely chopped
2 medium potatoes, peeled and chopped
2 celery sticks, chopped
1 large tomato, skinned and chopped
375 mℓ ribbon noodles, broken into small pieces
salt and pepper

Place the chicken, 3 ℓ of the water and chicken stock powder in the pot. Cover and simmer gently for 1 hour. Add the parsley, tarragon, bay leaves and onions and simmer for 30 minutes.

Add the potatoes, celery, tomato and remaining water. Simmer for another hour. Stir through occasionally.

Add the noodles and season with salt and pepper to taste. Simmer for a further 30 minutes. If the soup is too thick, dilute with water.

Vegetarian potjie

Arabian vegetarian potjie with bread and salad

If Colonel D.W. van Rooyen of Garsfontein, Pretoria, Chairman of the Northern Transvaal Potjiekos Guild, recommends a potjie, you can rest assured – it's bound to be a winner. He says: "This is a most unusual potjie. The ingredients are simple, yet the result is delicious." The recipe serves 4-6 people and we recommend two no. 3 pots.

375 mℓ brown lentils
750 mℓ water
375 mℓ uncooked rice
15 large onions, finely chopped
cooking oil
salt to taste

Bread

250 g cake flour
60 mℓ butter, cold and grated
80 mℓ water
salt to taste

Salad

carrots, coarsely grated
green peppers, chopped
cucumber, chopped
oil and lemon juice to taste
natural yoghurt

Rinse the lentils well, add the water and cook until nearly done in the pot. Add the rice and cook until done.

Fill the second pot halfway with oil and heat. Add the onions and deep-fry until just before they start burning. Spoon half the onions into the potjie with the lentil and rice mixture, adding 75 mℓ of the hot oil. Stir well and steam for approximately 15 minutes.

Spoon the remaining half of the onions into a suitable dish. Use the pot with the hot oil to make the pittas.

Sift the flour and add the butter, water and salt. Mix to a smooth dough. Roll out until quite thin. Using any shape the size of a saucer, cut the dough into rounds. Place the rounds in the hot oil and fry till golden.

In the meantime, prepare the salad: the quantities will be determined by the number of guests and the ingredients may be varied according to personal taste.

Spoon a serving of the lentil mixture into the bottom of a bowl and place some of the cooked onions on top. Spoon a serving of salad on top and garnish with yoghurt. Serve with the pitta.

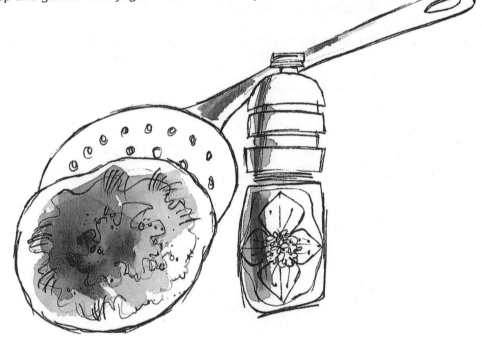

Side dishes

Whole-wheat bread

The recipe for this healthy bread was sent in by Mr P.W. Schutte of Chrismar, Bellville, in the Cape.

500 mℓ natural yoghurt
390 g whole-wheat flour
120 g cake flour
5 mℓ baking soda
5 mℓ brown sugar
5 mℓ baking powder
5 mℓ salt

Mix all the ingredients thoroughly. Shape the dough into a round bread and place in a well-greased flat-bottomed pot. Grease the lid and cover the pot with it. Bake the bread for approximately 1 hour over the coals, placing coals on top of the lid as well.

This bread can also be baked successfully in an oven of 200 °C for 1 hour. Cover the bread with tin foil after 30 minutes and bake for a further 30 minutes.

Baked sweet potatoes

The recipe for these mouthwatering sweet potatoes was sent in by Marita Botha of Middelburg in the Cape.

small sweet potatoes
cooking oil

Wash the sweet potatoes well. Dry them and coat the skins with a thin layer of cooking oil. Arrange them on a flat baking sheet and place in a hot oven at 200 °C and bake for 1 hour or longer until the sweet potatoes are soft when pinched between the thumb and forefinger. Follow the same procedure when baking the sweet potatoes in the coals, but wrap each one separately in foil. Also place some hot coals on top of the sweet potatoes.

Serve them whole, with or without butter.

Self-raising flour pot bread

The recipe for this flavoursome pot bread was sent in by Hester Beck of Springs.

1 packet (500 g) self-raising flour	
1 packet oxtail soup powder	
1 mℓ cayenne pepper	
125 mℓ grated Cheddar cheese	
500 mℓ buttermilk	

Mix all the ingredients and place in a greased flat-bottomed pot or a greased bread tin. Bake for approximately 1 hour amongst the coals or for 45 minutes in an oven at 180 °C (350 °F).

Potballetjies

Miemie Louw of De Hoek in the Cape sent us this most unusual recipe.

750 g cake flour
375 mℓ dried fruit cake mix
75 mℓ yellow sugar
10 mℓ salt
10 g instant dry yeast
5 mℓ mixed spice
75 mℓ butter
500 mℓ tepid rooibos tea

Combine the flour, dried fruit, yellow sugar, salt, instant dry yeast and mixed spice. Rub in the butter. Add the rooibos tea and knead until the mixture is manageable. Cover the dough with greased wax paper and leave in a warm spot. (Next to the fire is perfect, just be careful that the dough does not overheat. Turn the dish regularly to ensure that it becomes lukewarm right through.) Allow the dough to double in bulk.

Punch the dough down. Shape into balls and place them in a greased flat-bottomed pot. Grease the lid as well. Cover and allow the dough to rise until the pot is seven eighths full.

Pack some coals under the pot and on top of the lid, taking care not to overdo it – rather add some more coals later if the fire becomes too cold. Bake the balls, place in a dish and cover well with a cloth.

Mealie surprise

<table>
<tr><td>

Hint

Don't let a nasty wind spoil your potjie – protect it from dust by covering it with cabbage leaves.

</td></tr>
</table>

The ingredients might be humble, but the end result is a tasty surprise. Gerhard Fritz of Helderberg in the Cape is responsible for this recipe.

| 60 mℓ butter |
| 250 mℓ cake flour |
| 500 mℓ milk |
| 5 tins (410 g) mealie kernels, drained |
| 500 mℓ grated Cheddar cheese |

Melt the butter in the pot. Add the flour and stir until mixed. Remove from the coals and gradually add the milk. Return the pot to the coals, stirring the mixture continually until it comes to the boil. Add the mealies and mix well. Sprinkle the cheese on top and cover. Simmer very gently for about 1¼ hours. Do not stir. Garnish with chopped parsley.

French Parmesan cheese bread

This is a delicious alternative to run of the mill tomato and onion toasted sandwiches. Miss M.J. van Niekerk of Benoni sent us the recipe.

| 125 mℓ Parmesan cheese |
| 60 g soft butter |
| 6 slices French bread, cut approximately 2 cm thick |
| poppy seeds (optional) |

Mix the cheese and the butter, and spread the mixture on both sides of the bread. Sprinkle with poppy seeds if used. Place the slices on a grill over medium hot coals. Grill the bread on both sides until golden brown.

Willemien's vetkoek

Johan du Toit from Fauna in Bloemfontein sent us this recipe. His wife, Willemien, teaches at a special school and ever since she baked about 5 000 vetkoeke to increase their funds two years ago, there's been a standing order for her vetkoek at all the school functions.

72

2,5 kg cake flour	
10 mℓ salt	
1 cake (25 g) pressed yeast, crumbled	
5 mℓ sugar	
125 mℓ tepid water	
±2,5 ℓ tepid water	
100 mℓ cooking oil	
cooking oil for frying	

Sift the flour and salt together.

Mix the yeast, sugar and 125 mℓ tepid water and leave in a warm place for a while.

Make a hollow in the flour mixture. Pour the yeast mixture into the hollow and mix well. Knead in about 2,5 ℓ tepid water to form a manageable dough. Knead in the 100 mℓ cooking oil, kneading until the dough becomes elastic. Brush the dough with a little oil, cover and set aside in a warm place for 1 hour to rise.

Press the dough flat on a flat plate greased with oil. Cut out rounds, using, for example, an old jam tin. Fry the vetkoeke in hot oil until golden brown.

Health loaf

This fibre-packed currant loaf is a real winner. The recipe was sent in by Mrs B. Botha of Silverton, Pretoria.

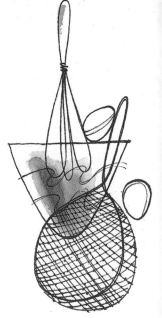

750 g cake flour	
100 g bran	
50 g Honey Crunch breakfast cereal	
45 mℓ baking powder	
40 g currants	
3 mℓ salt	
200 g margarine or butter	
1 egg	
50 mℓ brown sugar	
350 mℓ buttermilk	

Mix the flour, bran, breakfast cereal, baking powder, currants and salt. Melt the butter or margarine. Beat the egg and sugar and add to the dry ingredients. Add the melted butter or margarine. Add the buttermilk and mix to form a slack batter.

Spoon the mixture into a greased steamer or deep ovenproof dish, and cover tightly with the greased lid or paper. Place in a large pot with boiling water and steam for 2 hours. Allow to cool slightly. Turn out and serve with butter.

Special pot bread

This recipe, devised by Koos Myburgh and Gerhard Fritz of Helderberg in the Cape, looks and tastes equally good.

500 g self-raising flour
1 can beer
pinch salt
handful sunflower seeds
1 tin (410 g) mealie kernels, drained
handful grated cheese
1 medium onion, finely chopped
freshly chopped parsley
1 hard-boiled egg, mashed

Mix the self-raising flour, beer, salt, sunflower seeds and mealies. Knead thoroughly. Spoon the mixture into a flat-bottomed pot and cover with the lid. Set aside for 1 hour. If the sun is warm, leave the pot outside.

Make slits, two fingerwidths apart, across the top of the bread. Stuff the slits with cheese and onion. Sprinkle with parsley and bake in a preheated oven of 170 °C for 45 minutes. Garnish the loaf with egg once it is ready.

Whole-wheat pot bread

You won't regret trying the recipe for this deliciously wholesome pot bread, sent in by Annaleze Sieberhagen of Monte Vista in the Cape.

375 mℓ tepid water
50 mℓ golden syrup
20 mℓ dry yeast
750 mℓ white bread flour
750 mℓ whole-wheat flour
7 mℓ salt
75 mℓ cooking oil
100 mℓ tepid water

Mix the water and golden syrup. Add the yeast and wrap the dish warmly. Set the mixture aside until it forms a thick froth.

Sift the flour and salt together and return the bran remaining in the sieve to the flour mixture. Add the oil, little by little. Add the 100 mℓ tepid water and mix to form a soft, manageable dough. Knead well and wrap the dish in a cloth. Leave the dough to stand in a warm spot until it has doubled its bulk. Punch down.

Oil a pot and its lid thoroughly. Shape the dough into a round bread and place in the pot. Cover with the lid, wrap the pot warmly and leave the dough to rise until double its bulk.

Place the pot over the coals and put some coals on top of the lid. Bake the bread for 1 hour.

Steamed milk bread

Here's a recipe for an unusual pot bread, sent in by Mrs M.C. Cillié of Stellenbosch.

500 g self-raising flour
1 mℓ salt
310 mℓ milk

Combine all the ingredients and place the dough in a greased steamer or deep ovenproof dish. Cover tightly with the greased lid or paper and place in a large pot with boiling water. Steam for 2 hours. Cool slightly and turn out.

Whole-wheat beer bread

This recipe was sent in by Carl Liebenberg of Wendywood, Johannesburg. It's simple and therefore ideal to serve with any potjie.

600 mℓ beer
250 g whole-wheat flour
250 g cake flour
20 mℓ cream of tartar
10 mℓ baking soda
5 mℓ brown sugar
3 mℓ salt

Mix all the ingredients thoroughly and place the mixture in a well-greased flat-bottomed pot. Grease the lid and cover the pot with it. Bake the bread for approximately 1 hour over the coals, placing some coals on top of the lid as well.

Remove the pot from the coals and leave the bread to stand in the pot for 10 minutes. Turn out on a cloth. Serve with butter.

This bread can also be baked successfully in an oven of 200 °C for 1 hour. Cover the bread with tin foil after 30 minutes and bake for a further 30 minutes.

Lydia's raisin and aniseed pot bread

This delicious pot bread of Lydia Belcher of Bothasig won a first prize at the Boland Agricultural Show in 1986. We recommend a no. 8 pot.

825 m*l* tepid water	
5 m*l* white sugar	
20 m*l* dried yeast	
12 x 250 m*l* cake flour	
30 m*l* salt	
10 m*l* aniseed	
cooking oil to grease the pot and hands	
250 m*l* seedless raisins	

Dissolve the sugar in 125 m*l* tepid water. Stir in the yeast until dissolved. Cover the mixture with a saucer and leave to stand for approximately 10 minutes until it forms a thick froth.

Sift the flour and salt together and add the aniseed. Add the yeast mixture and enough water, little by little, to form a moist dough. Knead the dough for 10-15 minutes until it no longer sticks to the dish or hands. Grease the top of the dough with oil and cover with plastic cling wrap. Wrap the dish with the dough in a cloth and leave in a warm spot for about 2 hours until the dough has doubled in bulk.

Oil your hands and remove the dough from the dish. Punch down lightly and press raisins into the dough.

Oil a flat-bottomed pot and its lid. Place the dough in the pot, cover with the lid and wrap the pot in a cloth and leave to rise until the dough touches the lid of the pot.

Place the pot over the coals, cover the lid with a few coals and bake for 1 hour until an even brown. Remove the bread from the pot and wrap in a cloth.

André's pot bread

You'll hardly find an easier pot bread recipe than this one, sent in by André Swanepoel of Bellville.

500 g self-raising flour	
1 packet brown onion soup powder	
1 tin beer	
1 m*l* salt	

Combine all the ingredients and place in a greased flat-bottomed pot. Cover with the lid and bake in an oven of 180 °C for 45 minutes.

Fruit loaf

Although this loaf resembles a fruit cake, it is not quite as rich. The recipe was sent in by Mrs B. Botha of Silverton, Pretoria.

250 ml margarine or softened butter
250 ml brown sugar
4 eggs
875 ml cake flour
25 ml baking powder
2,5 ml salt
375 ml bran
250 ml buttermilk
375 ml fruit cake mix, including raisins, sultanas, currants and mixed fruit peel

Beat the margarine or butter and sugar until creamy. Beat the eggs and add to the butter or margarine mixture. Sift the flour, baking powder and salt together. Stir into the butter or margarine mixture, alternating it with the bran and buttermilk. Add the fruit mix and mix thoroughly.

Spoon the mixture into a greased steamer or deep ovenproof dish and cover tightly with the greased lid or paper. Place in a large pot with boiling water and steam for 2½ hours. Replenish the water with boiling water when necessary. Allow to cool slightly and turn out. Serve the loaf with butter.

Griddle cakes

No potjie is complete without some griddle cakes. Johan and Liz Shaw of Garsfontein, Pretoria, sent us this recipe.

500 ml self-raising flour
5 ml salt
1 egg
50 ml cooking oil
milk
water

Sift the flour and salt together. Break the egg in a 250 ml measuring cup and add the oil. Fill the cup to the 225 ml mark with a mixture of milk and water. Beat well.

Mix the flour and liquid to form a dough. Shape into little balls and flatten them slightly with your hand.

Bake the cakes for 12-15 minutes on a griddle over the coals, turning them once.

Beer griddle cakes

Pierre van Aswegen of Garsfontein, Pretoria, sent us this delicious, no-fuss recipe.

500 mℓ self-raising flour
5 mℓ salt
170 mℓ beer
tin foil, enough to cover the grill
cooking oil for coating the foil

Sift the flour and salt together. Add the beer and mix to form a smooth dough. Divide the dough into 6 equal parts. Roll each part into a ball and flatten slightly, using your hand. Fold a piece of foil over the grill, shiny side facing up. Grease the foil with the oil and arrange the griddle cakes on top. Fry the cakes on both sides until golden brown and done – approximately 20 minutes. Try to have the griddle cakes done in time to serve with the potjie.

Scottish griddle cakes

The oats in this recipe sent in by Philip Loots of Prince Alfred Hamlet, provide an interesting variation. Serve hot with butter and jam.

250 mℓ cake flour
10 mℓ baking powder
1 mℓ salt
125 mℓ margarine, at room temperature
375 mℓ oats
12,5 mℓ sugar
125 mℓ milk

Mix the flour, baking powder and salt together. Using the tips of your fingers, rub in the margarine. Add the oats and sugar. Make a hollow in the centre and add enough milk to form a soft dough.

Break off pieces of dough and roll into balls. Flatten the balls to form cakes approximately 1 cm thick. Bake on both sides on a hot, greased grill until golden brown and done.

Dessert

Date pot pudding

Colonel D.W. van Rooyen of Garsfontein, Pretoria, sent us this recipe. As with all his other recipes, this one, for which the colonel has won numerous first prizes, is bound to become a firm favourite.

Sauce

500 mℓ water
250 mℓ sugar
250 mℓ currants
30 mℓ grated orange peel
25 mℓ brandy

Batter

500 mℓ butter or margarine
250 mℓ castor sugar
1 egg
250 mℓ milk
10 mℓ baking soda
500 mℓ cake flour
10 mℓ ground ginger
5 mℓ ground cinnamon
2 mℓ salt
250 g dates
30 mℓ smooth apricot jam

Mix the sauce ingredients in a flat-bottomed pot.

Beat the butter or margarine and castor sugar until creamy. Beat the egg well and stir in.

Dissolve the baking soda in the milk. Sift the dry ingredients together and add to the butter or margarine mixture, alternating it with the milk. Add the dates and jam and mix thoroughly. Spoon the dough into the pot, along with the warm sauce. Cover with the lid and bake the pudding for approximately 1¼ hours over the coals, placing some coals on the lid.

Serve hot with cream or ice-cream. This pudding can also be made most successfully by baking it in a flat-bottomed pot in an oven of 180 °C for approximately 1 hour.

> **Hint**
> *A flat-bottomed pot is just right for puddings. Try making dumplings, date pudding or roly-poly in one – it works!*

Index